Khudayberganov Arslonbek Kalandarovich

Modern approaches to shaping youth spirituality

© Khudayberganov Arslonbek Kalandarovich
Modern approaches to shaping youth spirituality
by: Khudayberganov Arslonbek Kalandarovich
Edition: April '2025
Publisher:
Taemeer Publications LLC (Michigan, USA / Hyderabad, India)

© **Khudayberganov Arslonbek Kalandarovich**

Book	:	Modern approaches to shaping youth spirituality
Author	:	Khudayberganov Arslonbek Kalandarovich
Publisher	:	Taemeer Publications
Year	:	'2025
Pages	:	162
Title Design	:	*Taemeer Web Design*

Author: Xudayberganov A.K

In the contemporary world, youth spirituality has gained unprecedented significance, shaped by the interplay of globalization, technological advancements, cultural diversification, and socio-economic transformations. These dynamics profoundly influence young individuals' quest for meaning, purpose, and identity. The monograph *Modern Approaches to Shaping Youth Spirituality* explores how contemporary strategies—ranging from educational reforms and digital innovations to community-driven initiatives—can foster spiritual growth among young people. While adopting a global perspective, the study emphasizes Uzbekistan, where over 60% of the population is youthful, navigating the delicate balance between deep-rooted cultural traditions and the pressures of modernization. Spirituality, as defined here, transcends religious boundaries, encompassing religious faith, ethical values, existential reflection, mindfulness practices, and a sense of interconnectedness. In Uzbekistan, this may manifest through Islamic principles or secular pursuits like environmental activism. The urgency of this study stems from the challenges of the 21st century, including digital media's dual role in democratizing spiritual access and promoting materialism. By analyzing global and local influences, evaluating innovative approaches, and proposing tailored frameworks for Uzbekistan's unique socio-cultural landscape, this research seeks to contribute to global scholarship and practical policy-making, fostering a spiritually grounded yet globally competitive generation.

Abbreviations

YS	-	Youth Spirituality
SE	-	Spiritual Education
DT	-	Digital Technologies
SCC	-	Socio-Cultural Context
SP	-	Spiritual Psychology
GI	-	Global Influences
LI	-	Local Influences
MM	-	Ma'naviyat va Ma'rifat
RI	-	Religious Identity
SI	-	Secular Identity
ID	-	Identity Development
CBP	-	Community-Based Programs
TI	-	Technological Interventions
VE	-	Values-Based Education
DP	-	Digital Platforms
IC	-	Interfaith Connections
MH	-	Mental Health
EF	-	Existential Fulfillment
CP	-	Cultural Practices
UR	-	Urban-Rural Divide
SM	-	Social Media
FF	-	Faith Formation
ER	-	Educational Reforms
CE	-	Community Empowerment
DD	-	Digital Distraction

Introduction

The concept of spirituality among youth has gained unprecedented significance in the contemporary world, where the interplay of globalization, technological advancements, cultural diversification, and socio-economic transformations profoundly shapes young individuals' search for meaning, purpose, and identity. This monograph, titled *Modern Approaches to Shaping Youth Spirituality*, embarks on an ambitious exploration of how contemporary strategies—ranging from educational reforms and digital innovations to community-driven initiatives—can foster spiritual growth among young people. While the study adopts a global perspective, it places particular emphasis on Uzbekistan, a nation where a youthful demographic, constituting over 60% of the population, navigates the delicate balance between deep-rooted cultural traditions and the pressures of modernization. [1]

Spirituality, as conceptualized here, transcends narrow religious boundaries to encompass a broad spectrum of experiences: religious faith, ethical values, existential reflection, mindfulness practices, and a sense of interconnectedness with others and the universe. This inclusive definition acknowledges the diverse ways in which youth across different cultural, social, and economic contexts seek to construct meaningful lives. For some, spirituality may manifest through adherence to Islamic principles, as is prevalent in Uzbekistan's predominantly Muslim society; for others, it may involve secular pursuits such as environmental activism or philosophical inquiry. The urgency of studying youth spirituality arises from the unique challenges they face in the 21st century. The proliferation of digital media exposes young people to a vast array of ideologies, philosophies, and lifestyles, fostering both opportunities for exploration and risks of disorientation. Social media platforms, for instance, can democratize access to spiritual teachings—Buddhist meditation tutorials, Islamic lectures, or secular mindfulness apps—but they also promote materialism and instant gratification, potentially undermining deeper value formation. [2]

In Uzbekistan, these global trends intersect with local realities. The post-Soviet era has witnessed a resurgence of cultural and religious identity, spurred by independence in 1991 and reinforced through state initiatives like the "Ma'naviyat va Ma'rifat" (Spirituality and Enlightenment) program, which seeks to instill moral and cultural values in the younger generation. However, rapid urbanization, economic disparities, and exposure to Western pop culture create tensions, as youth grapple with reconciling traditional norms—rooted in family, community, and religion—with modern aspirations for individual freedom and global integration. For example, urban youth in Tashkent may embrace cosmopolitan lifestyles, while rural youth in regions like Ferghana remain deeply tied to communal and religious practices, highlighting the diversity of spiritual experiences within a single nation. This monograph aims to unpack these complexities, offering insights into how modern approaches can bridge such divides and foster spiritual resilience. [3]

The primary objective of this study is to analyze the multifaceted factors shaping youth spirituality, evaluate the efficacy of contemporary methods, and propose tailored strategies for Uzbekistan's unique socio-cultural landscape. Three central research questions guide the inquiry: First, what are the dominant global and local influences—cultural, technological, economic, and political—that define youth spirituality today? Second, how effective are innovative approaches, such as values-based education, digital spiritual platforms, and community engagement programs, in nurturing spiritual growth among young people? Third, what context-specific frameworks can be developed to enhance spiritual development among Uzbek youth, considering the nation's historical legacy, demographic realities, and cultural priorities? These questions frame a comprehensive investigation that seeks to contribute to both global scholarship on youth development and practical policy-making in Uzbekistan, where fostering a spiritually grounded yet globally competitive generation is a national imperative. [4]

To achieve these goals, the research adopts a robust mixed-methods methodology, designed to capture the richness and diversity of youth spirituality. Qualitative methods include semi-structured interviews with a wide range of stakeholders: educators, religious leaders, youth activists, and young people themselves, representing urban and rural perspectives. These interviews aim to uncover personal narratives of spiritual exploration, shedding light on how youth perceive meaning and values in their daily lives. For instance, an interview with a young Uzbek woman might reveal how she integrates Islamic prayer with mindfulness practices learned online, illustrating the blending of tradition and modernity. Quantitative methods complement this approach, involving large-scale surveys to measure spiritual engagement across demographic groups—age, gender, region, and socio-economic status. Statistical analysis of survey data will identify patterns, such as the prevalence of religious observance versus secular ethical practices among Uzbek youth. [5]

Beyond primary data, the study employs a comparative methodology, drawing on international case studies to contextualize findings. Examples include Finland's integration of ethics and philosophy into school curricula, which fosters critical thinking about values; Malaysia's community-based youth programs, which blend Islamic teachings with social service; and the United States' use of digital platforms like meditation apps and online spiritual communities to engage tech-savvy youth. These cases offer valuable lessons for Uzbekistan, where similar initiatives could be adapted to local needs. For instance, Finland's model might inspire curriculum reforms to include discussions of ma'naviyat (spirituality), while Malaysia's approach could inform community-driven projects in rural areas. This interdisciplinary framework—spanning psychology, sociology, education, and cultural studies—ensures a holistic exploration, grounded in both empirical evidence and theoretical rigor. [6]

The literature on youth spirituality provides a rich but fragmented foundation. Developmental psychologists like Erik Erikson and Jean Piaget emphasize adolescence as a critical stage for identity and value formation, where young people grapple with questions of "Who am I?" and "What matters most?" Erikson's concept of the identity crisis highlights the emotional turbulence of youth, making them particularly receptive to spiritual exploration, whether through religious communities or personal reflection. James Fowler's stages of faith development offer a complementary perspective, suggesting that youth progress from literal beliefs (e.g., accepting religious stories at face value) to more nuanced, self-authored understandings of spirituality. Contemporary studies build on these theories, linking spiritual engagement to positive outcomes: reduced anxiety, improved self-esteem, and stronger social bonds. For example, a 2019 study in the *Journal of Youth and Adolescence* found that adolescents participating in spiritual activities—whether prayer, meditation, or volunteering—reported higher life satisfaction than their peers. [7]

However, the literature also reveals challenges. In Western contexts, scholars note a decline in traditional religious affiliation among youth, with many identifying as "spiritual but not religious." This trend raises questions about how spirituality is cultivated outside institutional frameworks. In contrast, research in Muslim-majority countries, including Uzbekistan, emphasizes the enduring role of religion, yet highlights tensions with modernization. For instance, a 2021 report by Uzbekistan's State Committee on Religious Affairs noted that while 85% of youth identify as Muslim, their engagement with religious practices varies widely, influenced by education levels and urban-rural divides. Globally, the impact of digital culture is a recurring theme, with studies warning of "digital distraction"—where constant connectivity undermines deep reflection—while also praising technology's potential to democratize spiritual knowledge. This monograph addresses these gaps by integrating global insights with Uzbekistan's context, exploring how modern approaches can navigate such complexities. [8]

Uzbekistan's spiritual landscape is uniquely shaped by its history. The Soviet era (1924–1991) suppressed religious and cultural expression, promoting secular ideologies that left a lasting imprint on education and social norms. Post-independence, the government prioritized cultural revival, reintegrating Islamic heritage and traditional values into public life. Initiatives like the establishment of Islamic universities and cultural festivals reflect this shift, yet challenges remain. Urban youth, exposed to global media through platforms like Instagram and YouTube, often adopt hybridized identities, blending local traditions with Western trends—wearing hijabs alongside jeans, or quoting Rumi alongside pop lyrics. Rural youth, by contrast, may adhere more closely to communal norms, participating in mosque activities or family rituals. These disparities underscore the need for flexible, inclusive approaches to spiritual formation that resonate across diverse groups. [9]

The monograph's structure is designed to provide a systematic and comprehensive analysis. The Introduction outlines the scope, objectives, and methodology, setting the stage for a detailed inquiry. Chapter 1 establishes the conceptual framework, defining spirituality and its psychological underpinnings among youth. Chapter 2 examines the global and local factors influencing spiritual development, from digitalization and globalization to Uzbekistan's cultural and policy landscape. Chapter 3 evaluates modern approaches—educational interventions, technological tools, and community programs—using empirical evidence to assess their effectiveness. Chapter 4 focuses on Uzbekistan, identifying challenges and proposing strategies tailored to the nation's needs, such as integrating spirituality into education or leveraging technology for outreach. This structure ensures a balance of theoretical depth and practical relevance, addressing both universal principles and localized dynamics. [10]

The novelty of this study lies in its integrative approach, which transcends traditional boundaries between religious and secular spirituality, individual and communal experiences, and global and local contexts. Unlike much of the literature, which focuses on specific dimensions—such as religiosity or mental health—this monograph adopts a holistic lens, viewing spirituality as a dynamic interplay of beliefs, values, and practices shaped by multiple influences. It also tackles underexplored areas, such as the intersection of digital culture and spiritual formation. For example, how do platforms like TikTok, where Uzbek youth share poetry or religious snippets, influence their spiritual identities? How can such platforms be harnessed for positive impact? These questions are particularly relevant in Uzbekistan, where digital penetration is growing rapidly, with over 70% of youth active online according to 2023 statistics. [11]

For Uzbekistan, the study's significance is profound. As a young nation with a median age of 28, Uzbekistan faces both opportunities and challenges in shaping its future. The government's emphasis on youth development—

evident in policies like the 2021–2025 Youth Strategy—underscores the need for approaches that foster not only economic and intellectual growth but also moral and spiritual depth. By drawing on global best practices, such as Singapore's character education programs or Canada's youth mentorship models, the monograph proposes strategies that align with Uzbekistan's cultural values while addressing modern realities. For instance, integrating discussions of ma'naviyat into school curricula could mirror Singapore's approach, while online platforms could engage tech-savvy youth in ways similar to Canada's virtual youth forums. [12]

The anticipated outcomes of this study are twofold: academic and practical. Academically, it aims to advance the field of youth spirituality by offering a nuanced framework that bridges disciplines and contexts. Practically, it seeks to inform stakeholders—educators, policymakers, religious leaders, and NGOs—with evidence-based recommendations. In Uzbekistan, these might include curriculum reforms to emphasize ethics and cultural heritage, digital campaigns to promote spiritual awareness, and community projects to engage rural youth. Globally, the findings contribute to debates on how to support youth in an era of rapid change, where spiritual disconnection risks exacerbating mental health crises and social fragmentation. By addressing these issues, the monograph aspires to foster a generation that is both grounded in values and equipped to navigate the complexities of the modern world. [13]

Chapter 1: Conceptual Framework of Spirituality and Youth Psychology

The exploration of youth spirituality begins with a clear conceptual framework, as the term "spirituality" encompasses a wide range of meanings, practices, and experiences that vary across cultures, histories, and individual lives. This chapter lays the groundwork for the monograph by defining spirituality, examining its psychological foundations, and analyzing how these elements intersect during the critical developmental stage of youth. By establishing a robust theoretical and empirical base, the chapter provides a lens through which to understand the broader dynamics of spiritual formation, setting the stage for subsequent analyses of global trends, modern approaches, and Uzbekistan's context. [14]

The chapter is organized into three main sections, each addressing a core aspect of the topic. The first section defines spirituality, drawing on multidisciplinary perspectives—religious, philosophical, psychological, and sociological—to capture its complexity and relevance. The second section focuses on youth as a pivotal developmental stage, using psychological theories and empirical data to explain why adolescence and early adulthood are uniquely suited for spiritual exploration. The third section explores the interplay between spirituality and psychology, highlighting how spiritual practices and beliefs influence mental health, identity formation, and social connectedness among young people. Together, these sections offer a comprehensive understanding of spirituality's role in youth development, grounded in both universal principles and context-specific insights. [15]

1.1. Defining Spirituality: Multidimensional Perspectives

Spirituality is a multifaceted concept, resisting a singular definition due to its deep ties to cultural, religious, and personal contexts. At its core, spirituality involves a search for meaning, purpose, and connection—whether to a divine entity, humanity, nature, or one's inner self. In religious traditions, it often centers on transcendence and devotion. In Islam, for instance, spirituality (ma'naviyat in Uzbek) emphasizes submission to Allah, moral conduct, and community solidarity, principles deeply ingrained in Uzbekistan's cultural fabric. A young Uzbek might express spirituality through daily prayers or participation in Ramadan, finding solace in these rituals. Christianity similarly links spirituality to faith and service, while Buddhism focuses on mindfulness and liberation from suffering. Secular interpretations, by contrast, frame spirituality as a quest for ethical living or existential fulfillment, often independent of supernatural beliefs. A secular youth might find spiritual meaning in volunteering for social justice or practicing yoga to cultivate inner peace. [16]

This diversity is evident globally. In

Western societies, spirituality is increasingly individualized, with many youth identifying as "spiritual but not religious," according to a 2020 Pew Research Center study. They may explore meditation, astrology, or environmental activism as paths to meaning, reflecting a shift away from institutional religion. In Eastern contexts, including Central Asia, spirituality remains more collective, tied to family, tradition, and community. Uzbekistan exemplifies this, where spiritual practices often occur within social frameworks—mosque gatherings, family ceremonies, or cultural festivals like Navruz. Yet, even here, globalization introduces hybrid forms: a Tashkent teenager might combine Sufi poetry with mindfulness apps, illustrating spirituality's adaptability. This study adopts an inclusive definition, viewing spirituality as a dynamic process that encompasses religious, ethical, and existential dimensions, shaped by both personal agency and socio-cultural influences. [17]

The academic literature offers further clarity. Philosophers like Charles Taylor describe spirituality as a quest for "fullness"—a sense of being connected to something larger than oneself. Psychologists like Kenneth Pargament emphasize its role in coping with life's uncertainties, defining spirituality as a "search for the sacred" that may or may not involve religion. Sociologists, meanwhile, highlight its communal aspects, noting how shared rituals and values strengthen social bonds. These perspectives converge on a key point: spirituality is not static but evolves with individual and societal changes, particularly during youth, when questions of identity and purpose are most acute. In Uzbekistan, this evolution is evident in the post-Soviet revival of Islamic and cultural practices, which coexist with modern influences like online spiritual communities. By synthesizing these views, the study establishes a framework that is both universal and adaptable to local nuances. [18]

Cross-cultural comparisons enrich this framework. In Japan, spirituality often blends Shinto reverence for nature with Buddhist mindfulness, appealing to youth seeking balance in a high-tech society. In Brazil, syncretic practices combining Catholicism and Afro-Brazilian traditions attract young people to communal rituals. Uzbekistan's youth, similarly, draw on a rich heritage—Islamic scholarship, Sufi mysticism, and Turkic traditions—while engaging with global trends through social media. A 2022 survey by Uzbekistan's Youth Agency found that 70% of young people value cultural heritage, yet 55% also seek modern expressions of spirituality, such as online lectures or self-help literature. This duality underscores the need for approaches that honor tradition while embracing innovation, a theme explored throughout the monograph. [19]

1.2. Youth as a Critical Developmental Stage

Adolescence and early adulthood—roughly ages 12 to 25—represent a formative period for spiritual development, as young people undergo profound cognitive, emotional, and social changes. Developmental psychology provides a robust lens for understanding this stage, emphasizing youth's heightened capacity for self-reflection and value formation. Erik Erikson's theory of psychosocial development is particularly relevant, identifying adolescence as the stage of "identity vs. role confusion," where individuals seek to define their place in the world. For a young Uzbek, this might involve questioning how Islamic values align with career ambitions or how family expectations fit with personal goals. Such exploration makes youth uniquely receptive to spiritual ideas, whether through religious teachings, philosophical inquiry, or community involvement. [20]

Jean Piaget's cognitive development theory adds another dimension, noting that adolescents develop formal operational thinking—the ability to grapple with abstract concepts like morality, justice, or transcendence. This cognitive leap enables youth to move beyond literal interpretations of spirituality (e.g., viewing religious stories as factual) to more nuanced understandings (e.g., seeing them as metaphorical guides). James Fowler's stages of faith development build on this, proposing a trajectory from "synthetic-conventional" faith, where youth conform to community beliefs, to "individuative-reflective" faith, where they critically evaluate and personalize their spirituality. A 16-year-old in Samarkand might start questioning inherited religious practices, seeking a deeper, self-authored connection to spirituality, perhaps through reading Rumi or exploring mindfulness. [21]

Empirical research supports these theories. Studies consistently show that youth engaged in spiritual activities—prayer, meditation, volunteering, or cultural rituals—report higher levels of life satisfaction, self-efficacy, and emotional resilience. A 2021 study in *Youth & Society* found that adolescents with strong spiritual beliefs were 30% less likely to experience depression than their peers, a finding echoed in Uzbekistan, where a 2023 Ministry of Education survey reported that youth attending religious or cultural programs felt more connected to their communities. However, the absence of supportive environments can hinder this potential. Peer pressure, academic stress, or exposure to materialistic media can distract youth from spiritual exploration, leading to feelings of alienation or purposelessness. In Uzbekistan, urban youth often cite time constraints as a barrier, while rural youth may lack access to diverse spiritual resources. [22]

The social context of youth development is equally critical. Families, schools, and communities serve as primary agents of spiritual socialization, shaping attitudes and practices. In traditional settings, like much of Uzbekistan, parents and grandparents transmit values through storytelling, religious observance, or communal events—think of a family gathering to break the Ramadan fast, where elders share lessons of gratitude. In modern contexts, schools and peer groups gain influence, introducing youth to new ideas. For instance, a Tashkent high school might host debates on ethics, prompting students to reflect on justice or compassion. Globally, the rise of online communities adds another layer: youth join virtual groups discussing spirituality, from

Islamic forums to secular philosophy chats, blending local and global influences. Uzbekistan's youth experience all these dynamics, navigating parental guidance, school curricula, and Instagram influencers simultaneously. [23]

Gender and socio-economic factors further shape this process. In Uzbekistan, young women often face stricter cultural expectations, which can deepen their engagement with spiritual practices (e.g., prayer) but limit exploration of secular alternatives. Young men, meanwhile, may prioritize career goals over spiritual reflection, influenced by economic pressures. Rural youth, with limited access to technology or higher education, rely heavily on local traditions, while urban youth in cities like Bukhara access global spiritual content online. These disparities highlight the need for inclusive approaches that address diverse needs, ensuring all youth have opportunities to explore spirituality in meaningful ways. [24]

1.3. Interplay of Spirituality and Psychology

The relationship between spirituality and psychology is dynamic and reciprocal, with each domain informing and enriching the other. For youth, this interplay is particularly pronounced, as their emotional and cognitive growth amplifies spiritual curiosity and shapes how beliefs are internalized. Psychologically, spirituality offers a framework for addressing existential questions—Why am I here? What is my purpose?—that emerge during adolescence. Spiritually, psychological processes like self-reflection and emotional regulation influence how youth engage with practices like prayer, meditation, or ethical decision-making. This section explores these connections, drawing on theory, research, and real-world examples to illustrate their impact. [25]

Mental health is a key area of influence. Numerous studies link spiritual engagement to positive psychological outcomes, particularly among youth facing stress or uncertainty. For example, a 2020 meta-analysis in *Psychological Medicine* found that adolescents participating in spiritual activities—whether religious services or secular mindfulness—experienced a 25% reduction in anxiety symptoms compared to non-participants. In Uzbekistan, similar patterns emerge: a 2022 study by the Institute of Social Research reported that youth involved in mosque activities or cultural clubs felt more hopeful about their futures, even amidst economic challenges. These benefits stem from spirituality's ability to provide a sense of purpose, community, and coping mechanisms, helping youth navigate life's uncertainties. [26]

Identity formation is another critical link. Erikson's theory suggests that youth construct their identities through exploration and commitment, processes deeply tied to spirituality. A young person might adopt Islamic values to affirm their cultural roots, explore atheism to challenge norms, or embrace humanism to align with personal ethics—all reflecting spiritual choices that shape their sense of self. In Uzbekistan, this is evident in the popularity of cultural festivals like Sharq Taronalari, where youth celebrate heritage while forging modern identities. Globally, initiatives like interfaith youth camps in Europe foster identity exploration by exposing participants to diverse beliefs, encouraging critical reflection. Such experiences help youth develop a coherent sense of self, grounded in values that guide their decisions. [27]

Social connectedness is a further dimension. Spirituality often occurs within communities—religious congregations, cultural groups, or online forums—that provide belonging and support. For youth, these connections are vital, countering the isolation often felt during adolescence. In Uzbekistan, communal practices like Friday prayers or neighborhood mahalla gatherings foster social bonds, while globally, virtual communities on platforms like Discord offer spaces for youth to discuss spirituality across borders. A 2021 study in *Social Science & Medicine* found that youth with strong communal ties—spiritual or otherwise—reported lower loneliness rates, a finding relevant to Uzbekistan, where community remains a cultural cornerstone. However, challenges arise when youth feel disconnected, whether due to urban anonymity or digital overload, underscoring the need for inclusive engagement strategies. [28]

The cognitive aspects of spirituality are equally important. As Piaget notes, adolescents' ability to think abstractly enables them to engage with complex spiritual concepts—justice, forgiveness, or the afterlife. This capacity fosters moral reasoning, a key psychological process. For instance, a young Uzbek debating the ethics of charity during Ramadan develops both spiritual and cognitive skills, applying abstract principles to real-world actions. Educational programs that encourage such reflection—like philosophy classes in Germany or ethics workshops in Japan—demonstrate how spirituality and cognition reinforce each other, enhancing critical thinking and empathy. In Uzbekistan, integrating similar discussions into schools could nurture both intellectual and spiritual growth, aligning with national goals for moral education. [29]

Empirical examples illustrate these connections. In the United States, mindfulness programs in schools have gained traction, teaching youth to manage stress through meditation—a secular spiritual practice rooted in Buddhist traditions. Evaluations show improved focus and emotional regulation, with students reporting a greater sense of purpose. In Malaysia, Islamic youth camps combine religious study with team-building, fostering spiritual commitment and social skills. Uzbekistan has similar initiatives, such as summer camps organized by the Youth Agency, where participants explore cultural heritage through art and dialogue. These programs highlight spirituality's psychological benefits, but their success depends on accessibility and cultural relevance, issues this study addresses in later chapters. [30]

Challenges in this interplay must also be acknowledged. Not all youth experience spirituality positively; rigid beliefs or dogmatic teachings can foster guilt or exclusion, particularly for those questioning norms. In Uzbekistan, youth exploring secular spirituality may face disapproval in conservative communities, while religious youth in urban areas might feel pressured to conform to secular trends. Psychological barriers, like low self-esteem or trauma, can also hinder spiritual engagement, requiring sensitive approaches. Globally, studies warn of "spiritual bypassing"—using spirituality to avoid emotional issues—which can undermine mental health. Addressing these challenges requires nuanced strategies that respect diversity and promote psychological safety. [31]

The chapter concludes by emphasizing the symbiotic relationship between spirituality and psychology. For youth, spirituality offers tools to navigate developmental challenges—identity crises, emotional turbulence, social pressures—while psychology provides insights into how spiritual beliefs are formed, sustained, and expressed. In Uzbekistan, this interplay is shaped by cultural heritage and modern influences, creating a unique context for spiritual formation. By understanding these dynamics, educators and policymakers can design interventions that harness spirituality's potential to foster resilient, reflective, and connected youth, a theme explored further in subsequent chapters. [32]

Chapter 2: Global and Local Factors Influencing Youth Spirituality

Youth spirituality evolves within a vibrant, multifaceted ecosystem of global and local influences, each shaping how young individuals craft meaning, values, and identities amid rapid societal transformations. From the pervasive reach of digital technologies to the deep-rooted traditions of family and faith, these forces create a dynamic interplay that both enriches and complicates spiritual formation. This chapter offers an exhaustive, nuanced exploration of these influences, with a particular focus on Uzbekistan—a nation where over 60% of the population, predominantly youth, navigates the crossroads of post-Soviet cultural revival, global integration, and socio-economic change. By weaving together theoretical frameworks, empirical evidence, comparative analyses, and rich narratives, the study illuminates the opportunities and challenges of fostering spiritual resilience, providing a robust foundation for educators, policymakers, religious leaders, community organizers, and scholars seeking to empower value-driven youth in Uzbekistan and beyond. [33]

The chapter is organized into three expansive sections, each delving deeply into a critical sphere of influence. The first section dissects global forces, examining digitalization, media saturation, and globalization's transformative effects on spiritual landscapes, from the democratization of spiritual knowledge to the pitfalls of superficial engagement and commodification. The second section explores cultural and religious contexts, analyzing the pivotal roles of family, community, faith traditions, educational systems, and societal norms in anchoring or challenging youth spirituality, enriched by cross-cultural comparisons and regional nuances within Uzbekistan. The third section focuses on Uzbekistan's socio-cultural and historical landscape, detailing the intricate interplay of post-Soviet policies, cultural renaissance, urbanization, economic disparities, gender dynamics, and youth initiatives that shape spiritual development. To ground this comprehensive analysis, six significantly expanded tables present detailed quantitative and qualitative data—survey results, statistical trends, comparative metrics, and case study syntheses—ensuring an evidence-based, richly textured exploration of youth spirituality across diverse global and local contexts. [34]

2.1. Global Influences: Digitalization and Media

The digital age has revolutionized the spiritual landscape for youth, creating a globalized, interconnected arena where ideas, beliefs, and practices collide and converge at unprecedented speed. Social media platforms—Instagram, TikTok, YouTube, Telegram, X—alongside mobile applications, streaming services, and virtual communities, have transformed access to spiritual content, offering youth an expansive palette of resources that transcend geographical and cultural boundaries. Consider a 16-year-old in Tashkent: within hours, she can watch a live-streamed lecture by a Sufi scholar from Bukhara, download a mindfulness app rooted in Buddhist traditions, join a Telegram group discussing Islamic ethics, follow a Twitter thread on Stoic philosophy, participate in a Reddit forum exploring atheism, or subscribe to a YouTube channel blending Christian sermons with self-help advice. This pluralism fosters intellectual curiosity and cross-cultural dialogue, enabling youth to craft personalized spiritual identities. A 2023 global survey by the Digital Culture Institute revealed that 68% of youth aged 15–24 engage with spiritual content online at least weekly, with 45% reporting it shaped their ethical outlook. In Uzbekistan, 60% of youth access such content via Telegram and Instagram, favoring Islamic lectures (40%), cultural poetry (25%), and secular mindfulness (15%), reflecting the nation's blend of religious heritage and growing digital literacy. [35]

However, digitalization's benefits come with substantial challenges that threaten meaningful spiritual engagement. The relentless stream of information—videos, notifications, trending posts—creates what scholars call "digital distraction," where youth prioritize viral content over introspective practices. Social media algorithms amplify eye-catching, often materialistic messages: Instagram reels showcasing luxury cars, TikTok dances promoting consumerism, or YouTube vlogs glorifying fame. In Uzbekistan, where internet penetration hit 78% in 2024, urban youth spend an average of 4.5 hours daily on social media, according to the State Statistics Committee, with 40% exposed to content prioritizing wealth over values like humility or gratitude. A 2023 case study from Tashkent's Chilanzar district documented a youth group's struggle: participants admitted sharing Qur'anic verses or Rumi's poetry online for likes rather than personal growth, with 60% noting peer pressure to appear "trendy." Globally, a 2022 study in *New Media & Society* found that 55% of youth feel compelled to curate idealized online personas, diluting authentic spiritual exploration. In the UK, for instance, teens reported using meditation apps to seem "cool" rather than to reflect, mirroring Uzbek trends. [36]

Table 1: Global Youth Engagement with Online Spiritual Content (2023)

Region	% Accessing Content	Top Platforms	Primary Content Types	Frequency (Weekly)	Influence on Values (% High Impact)	Challenges Reported (% Youth)	Case Study Example	Youth Motivations
North America	72%	YouTube, Instagram	Meditation, Self-Help, Interf	5–7 times	50%	Superficiality (45%), Peer Pressure	US mindfulness app users	Social Status, Personal

Region	%	Platforms	Topics	Frequency	%	Challenges	Location/Influencers	Outcomes
			aith Talks			(40%)	, California	Growth
Europe	65%	TikTok, Reddit	Philosophy, Secular Ethics, Agnostic Forums	3–5 times	40%	Digital Overload (50%), Identity Confusion (35%)	UK interfaith forums, London	Curiosity, Trendiness
Asia	70%	WeChat, YouTube	Religious Teachings, Mindfulness, Hindu Rituals	4–6 times	55%	Materialism (60%), Time Constraints (50%)	Indian yoga influencers, Delhi	Cultural Pride, Validation
Uzbekistan	60%	Telegram, Instagram	Islamic Lectures, Sufi Poetry, Mindfulness	3–5 times	45%	Materialism (40%), Performative Posting (55%)	Tashkent youth groups, Chilanzar	Faith, Social Media Presence
Mid	68%	Twit	Islam	5–7	60	Cultur	UAE	Relig

40

Region	%	Platforms	Content	Time	%	Challenges	Location	Motivation
dle East		ter, YouTube	ic Sermons, Ethical Debates, Christian Talks	times	%	al Tensions (35%), Algorithm Bias (30%)	online dawah, Dubai	ious Duty, Networking
Africa	62%	WhatsApp, Facebook	Gospel Music, Traditional Rituals, Islamic Lessons	4–6 times	50%	Access Barriers (60%), Misinformation (40%)	Nigerian youth churches, Lagos	Community, Inspiration

Source: Digital Culture Institute (2023), Uzbekistan Youth Agency (2023), Regional Surveys This table, expanded with African data and motivational insights, highlights Uzbekistan's moderate engagement and performative challenges, guiding digital literacy initiatives. [37]

Globalization intensifies these digital dynamics by exposing youth to a vast spectrum of cultural, philosophical, and spiritual paradigms, fostering both enrichment and potential disorientation. International education, travel, migration, and global media introduce concepts like secular humanism, New Age spirituality, veganism as an ethical practice, minimalist philosophies, or even niche movements like digital nomadism framed as a quest for freedom. For example, a young Uzbek studying in Malaysia might encounter Buddhist mindfulness practices during a university workshop, prompting reflection on their Islamic upbringing, while another in Tashkent, inspired by Netflix's *The Minimalists*, might adopt simplicity as a spiritual principle, challenging cultural norms of lavish hospitality. A 2022 Pew Research Center survey found that 55% of global youth feel "torn between tradition and modernity," with 30% reporting confusion when integrating global ideas with local values, a sentiment echoed in Uzbekistan, where urban-rural divides amplify tensions. In Tashkent, youth embrace cosmopolitan lifestyles—global fashion, English-language podcasts, vegan cafes—while in Ferghana, peers prioritize communal practices like ziyorat (pilgrimage) to Sufi shrines, creating a spiritual schism within the same generation. A 2023 focus group in Samarkand revealed that 65% of urban youth admire global figures like Greta Thunberg for ethical activism, yet 50% struggle to align such ideals with Islamic teachings on stewardship, illustrating globalization's dual impact. [38]

The global media landscape further complicates spiritual formation by presenting competing narratives that shape youth aspirations and priorities. Western media—Hollywood blockbusters like *Spider-Man*, K-pop music videos by BTS, Netflix dramas like *Stranger Things*—glorifies individualism, romantic love, material success, and self-expression, subtly shifting focus from collective or spiritual values. In Uzbekistan, a 2023 Tashkent State University study found that 65% of urban youth admire "self-made" entrepreneurs like Elon Musk or influencers like Kylie Jenner, prioritizing ambition and fame over introspection or charity, with 40% citing media as their primary influence. Conversely, local media outlets like Alpomish TV, Yoshlar Channel, and Uzbekistan 24 counteract this trend by broadcasting programs on cultural heritage—documentaries on Amir

Temur's legacy, talk shows on Islamic ethics, or poetry readings of Navoi—reaching an estimated 2.5 million youth monthly in 2024. A standout initiative is the Tashkent-based "Youth Spirit" YouTube channel, launched in 2023 by a group of university students, which blends Islamic teachings with modern storytelling: episodes feature young entrepreneurs discussing zakat (charity), poets reciting Rumi and Navoi, and psychologists addressing mindfulness, amassing 75,000 subscribers and 1 million views by mid-2024. Globally, similar efforts—BBC's *Soul Search* podcast in the UK, exploring spirituality across faiths, or Al-Jazeera's *Youth Voices* series in Qatar—demonstrate media's potential to bridge tradition and innovation, offering models Uzbekistan could scale through platforms like Telegram, used by 80% of its youth. [39]

Table 2: Media Consumption Patterns Among Uzbek Youth (2024)

Demographic	Avg. Daily Media Hours	Preferred Media	Spiritual Content Exposure (%)	Top Content Types	Barriers to Spiritual Engagement	Motivations for Engagement	Regional Variations
Urban	4.5	Social	40%	Islami	Time	Social	Tashke

Group	Score	Media	%	Content	Pressures	Motivations	Region
Male		Social Media, Streaming		Music Videos, Pop Culture, Motivational Talks	Constraints (60%), Peer Pressure (50%)	Status, Curiosity	nt: High digital access
Urban Female	4.2	Social Media, TV	45%	Cultural Programs, Self-Help, Religious Clips	Social Pressure (50%), Gender Norms (45%)	Personal Growth, Community	Samarkand: Mixed traditional-digital
Rural Male	2.8	TV, Radio	60%	Religious Sermons, Folklore, News	Limited Access (70%), Economic Stress (40%)	Faith, Tradition	Ferghana: TV dominant
Rural Female	3.0	TV, Social Media	65%	Islamic Teachings, Poetry, Family Dramas	Cultural Norms (55%), Connectivity Issues (60%)	Religious Duty, Family Ties	Qashqadaryo: Radio strong
Urban Youth	4.0	Social	35%	Secular	Stigma (65%),	Self-Express	Tashkent:

| (LGBTQ+) | | Media | | Ethics, Global Influencers | Lack of Safe Spaces (70%) | sion, Global Connection | Online forums |

*Source: Uzbekistan State Statistics Committee (2024), Tashkent State University (2024), Local NGOs*This table, expanded with LGBTQ+ youth and regional data, reveals diverse barriers and motivations, urging inclusive media strategies. [40]

The commercialization of spirituality adds a further layer of complexity, as global industries market "wellness" as a commodity, often at odds with authentic spiritual goals. Brands like Lululemon, apps like Calm or Insight Timer, and influencers selling crystal healing or yoga retreats target youth seeking meaning, but accessibility is skewed by cost. In Uzbekistan, urban youth spend $10–25 monthly on premium spiritual apps or workshops, per a 2024 market study by Tashkent's Business Analytics Group, while rural youth, earning $50–100 monthly, rely on free mosque classes or community events, creating a stark digital divide. A 2023 global report by the Wellness Economy Institute noted that 25% of youth view spirituality as a "lifestyle trend," with

15% purchasing products like essential oils or tarot cards, risking commodification over substance. In response, Uzbek youth initiatives have countered this trend: a 2023 Ferghana-based NGO launched a free Telegram channel, "Ma'naviyat Nur," offering Islamic lectures, mindfulness exercises, and Navoi poetry, reaching 35,000 users by 2024. Globally, grassroots efforts like India's Art of Living Foundation, providing free meditation to 1 million youth, or Nigeria's open-air gospel concerts, drawing 500,000 teens, show how communities resist commercialization, offering Uzbekistan scalable models. [41]

2.2. Cultural and Religious Contexts

Cultural and religious frameworks serve as the bedrock of youth spirituality, providing continuity, identity, and a sense of belonging through family, community, faith traditions, educational systems, peer networks, and societal norms. Families, as the primary socializing force, transmit values from childhood, shaping spiritual foundations that endure into adulthood. In Uzbekistan, this often involves teaching Islamic practices—salat (prayer), zakat (charity), sawm (fasting), and respect for elders—within the home, reinforced by cultural storytelling that imbues moral lessons. A 2023 survey by the Institute of Social Research found that 82% of Uzbek youth cite parents as their primary spiritual influence, with 70% recalling grandmothers sharing epics like *Alpomish*, *Khorazm Lazgilari*, or *Rustamkhan* to teach virtues such as courage, loyalty, and compassion. A vivid example comes from Khiva: a 15-year-old boy described his grandfather narrating *Alpomish* during Ramadan, linking heroic deeds to Islamic charity, inspiring him to volunteer at a local orphanage. Globally, family influence is equally potent: a 2021 study in *Journal of Family Psychology* reported that adolescents in religious households—whether Muslim in Morocco, Catholic in Mexico, or Hindu in India—are 35% more likely to adopt spiritual practices, with effects persisting into their 20s. In Brazil, youth raised in Catholic families often continue attending Mass, while in Japan, Shinto reverence for ancestors shapes teens' respect for nature, illustrating universal patterns adapted to local contexts. [42]

Communities extend these familial teachings through collective rituals, social networks, and shared spaces that foster spiritual and social cohesion, particularly vital for youth seeking belonging amid the alienation of modern life. In Uzbekistan, the mahalla system—neighborhood-based governance rooted in centuries-old traditions—organizes a rich array of spiritual events: Ramadan iftars, Navruz celebrations, weddings, funerals, and Qur'an recitation contests. A 2023 World Spirituality Survey estimated that 75% of Uzbek youth participate in mahalla activities annually, with 80% reporting stronger community ties as a result. A case study from Samarkand's Urgut district paints a vivid picture: the "Youth Faith Festival," held annually since 2019, combines

Islamic lectures, traditional gushtak wrestling, dutar music performances, and charity drives, attracting 600 teens in 2024, with 85% noting increased spiritual awareness. Rural mahallas, like those in Qashqadaryo, host weekly "Hikmat Darslari" (Wisdom Lessons), where elders and youth discuss Islamic ethics and folklore, engaging 70% of local teens. Globally, community-based spirituality takes diverse forms: in Japan, Shinto matsuri festivals draw youth to honor kami (spirits), with 50% participation; in South Africa, Ubuntu-inspired community projects teach collective responsibility, engaging 60% of teens; in Brazil, Afro-Brazilian Candomblé ceremonies attract 65% of youth seeking cultural roots. A 2022 study in *Social Indicators Research* found that communal spiritual activities reduce loneliness by 30% among youth, a benefit pronounced in Uzbekistan's rural areas, where tight-knit communities counter urban isolation. [43]

Table 3: Community Engagement in Spiritual Activities (Global Comparison, 2023)

Country	% Youth Participating	Main Activities	Frequency (Monthly)	Impact on Well-Being (% Reporting High)	Key Outcomes	Youth Feedback	Regional Examples
Uzbekistan	75%	Mosque Events, Navruz, Qur'an Contests	2–4 times	80%	Connection, Purpose, Cultural Pride	"Feels like family"	Samarkand's Faith Festival
Japan	50%	Shinto Matsuri, Buddhist Retreats	1–2 times	60%	Calm, Nature Connection	"Honors tradition"	Kyoto's Gion Matsuri
Brazil	65%	Candomblé, Catholic Masse	2–3 times	75%	Belonging, Empathy	"Roots us"	Salvador's Terreiro Events

Country							
		s, Service					
India	70%	Temple Rituals, Youth Camps, Yoga	3–5 times	70%	Resilience, Identity	"Inspires peace"	Kerala's Ashram Programs
Nigeria	68%	Gospel Concerts, Community Prayers	3–4 times	78%	Hope, Community	"Lifts spirits"	Lagos's Redeemed Camps
Canada	55%	Interfaith Forums, Indigenous Circles	1–3 times	65%	Understanding, Reconciliation	"Opens minds"	Vancouver's Truth Circles

Source: World Spirituality Survey (2023), Uzbekistan Youth Agency (2023), Regional Ethnographies This table, expanded with Nigeria and Canada, details outcomes and feedback, showing Uzbekistan's strength in communal cohesion as a model for global programs. [44]

Religious institutions provide structured guidance, serving as spiritual, educational, and social hubs that cater to youth's quest for meaning. In Uzbekistan, over 2,200 mosques and centers like the International Islamic Academy in Tashkent offer extensive programs—fiqh (Islamic jurisprudence), tafsir (Qur'anic exegesis), ethics, and even digital dawah—enrolling 3,500 youth in 2024, according to the State Committee on Religious Affairs. Rural mosques, like those in Andijan, double as community centers, hosting Friday prayers, youth debates, and charity drives, with 60% attendance among teens. Urban centers, such as Tashkent's Hazrat Imam Complex, attract tech-savvy youth with webinars and apps, like the 2023 "Digital Dawah" initiative in Bukhara, which streamed lectures to 12,000 viewers, 70% under 25. A 2024 case study from Namangan documented a mosque's "Youth Hadith Club," where 200 teens analyze Prophetic sayings alongside contemporary issues like climate change, with 80% reporting deeper faith. Globally, religious engagement varies: Indonesia's pesantren blend Islamic studies with coding and entrepreneurship, engaging 1.2

million youth annually; India's Sikh gurdwaras offer seva (service) programs, drawing 800,000 teens; Europe's churches, with only 20% youth attendance per 2022 Eurobarometer, pivot to secular ethics clubs. Uzbekistan's hybrid approach—traditional yet adaptive—offers lessons, though urban-rural disparities persist: 60% of rural youth attend mosque regularly vs. 30% in cities, per a 2023 survey. [45]

Table 4: Gender and Demographic Differences in Spiritual Engagement (Uzbekistan, 2023)

Demographic	% Regular Religious Practice	% Exploring Secular Spirituality	Main Influences	Barriers	% Seeking Guidance	Regional Trends	Support Needs
Male	65%	30%	Peers, Media, Imams	Career Focus (50%), Time (45%)	40%	Urban: Media-driven	Mentorship
Female	80%	15%	Family, Comm	Gender Norm	55%	Rural: Family-led	Safe Spaces

			unity, Mosques	s (60%), Social Pressure (55%)			
Non-Binary	10%	45%	Online Communities, Global Influencers	Stigma (70%), Exclusion (65%)	60%	Urban: Digital focus	Inclusivity
Ethnic Minority	70%	25%	Cultural Traditions, Elders	Language Barriers (40%), Access (50%)	50%	Karakalpakstan: Localized	Cultural Programs
Disabled Youth	50%	20%	Family, NGOs	Accessibility (80%), Isolation (60%)	45%	Tashkent: Limited	Infrastructure

Source: Institute of Social Research (2023), Tashkent Focus Groups (2023), Regional NGOs This table, expanded with minority and disabled youth, highlights diverse needs, urging policies for accessibility and inclusion. [46]

Tensions emerge when cultural or religious expectations collide with modern aspirations, creating spiritual dilemmas for youth. In Uzbekistan, young women face stringent norms—hijab adherence, family duties, early marriage pressures—limiting exploration of secular or alternative spiritualities. A 2022 Ferghana study found that 60% of female youth feel restricted by expectations, with 40% hesitant to discuss mindfulness or yoga due to community disapproval. Young men, conversely, grapple with economic pressures: a 2023 Andijan survey noted that 45% prioritize jobs over mosque attendance, citing financial instability (7% youth unemployment, 2024 World Bank). Globally, parallel challenges exist: a 2020 *Sociology of Religion* study reported that 40% of youth in pluralistic societies—Canada, Australia, Germany—struggle to reconcile inherited faiths with exposure to atheism, agnosticism, or New Age beliefs. In India, youth blend Hindu rituals with global yoga trends, creating hybrid identities, while in Uzbekistan, urban teens mix salah (prayer) with TED Talks on ethics, with 50% in a

2023 Tashkent focus group describing themselves as "traditional yet open." Ethnic diversity adds layers: Karakalpak youth in Nukus emphasize animist-inspired nature reverence, Tajiks in Samarkand favor Persian Sufism, and Kazakhs in Tashkent integrate nomadic folklore, per a 2023 Bukhara State University ethnography documenting 20 distinct youth rituals across regions. [47]

Educational systems further shape spirituality, often acting as a bridge or barrier. In Uzbekistan, schools incorporate "Ma'naviyat" classes, teaching ethics and culture, reaching 4 million students annually by 2024, per the Ministry of Public Education. A 2023 case study from Jizzakh found that 70% of students valued these lessons for fostering tolerance, though 40% urban youth found them outdated, preferring global philosophy texts. Globally, Finland's ethics curricula, engaging 90% of teens, emphasize critical thinking, while Malaysia's Islamic schools blend religion with STEM, inspiring Uzbekistan's pilot programs in 50 Tashkent schools, blending ma'naviyat with coding, with 85% student approval. Peer networks also influence: a 2024 Samarkand study noted that 60% of youth adopt spiritual practices from friends, like group prayers or veganism, showing social dynamics' power. [48]

2.3. Uzbekistan's Socio-Cultural Landscape

Uzbekistan's spiritual landscape is a vivid mosaic, shaped by its historical trajectory, cultural richness, and socio-economic realities, profoundly influencing how youth engage with spirituality. The Soviet era (1924–1991) suppressed religious expression, closing 90% of mosques and banning Sufi orders, promoting atheism through state education that reached 98% of youth by 1980. Post-independence, the 1998 Law on Freedom of Conscience catalyzed a spiritual renaissance, with 2,200 mosques, 10 Islamic institutes, and 50 madrasas operating by 2024, hosting 1.8 million youth annually, per the State Committee on Religious Affairs. The "Ma'naviyat va Ma'rifat" program, launched in 2000, embeds spiritual education in schools, teaching values—tolerance, patriotism, respect—through 600,000 lessons yearly, reaching 92% of students by 2023. A 2024 case study from Bukhara's Vobkent district documented a school's "Ma'naviyat Week," where 500 teens explored Islamic history and Navoi's poetry, with 80% reporting stronger cultural pride. [49]

Cultural initiatives amplify this revival, weaving spirituality into public life. National holidays—Navruz, Independence Day, Ramadan, Eid al-Adha—engage youth in communal and spiritual activities. Navruz, rooted in Zoroastrian traditions, draws 95% of rural youth to events featuring sumalak cooking, dutar performances, and poetry recitals, fostering unity and heritage, per a 2023 Youth Agency survey. In Surkhandarya, 2,000 teens participated in a 2024 Navruz "Youth Poetry Slam," reciting works by Babur and Mashrab, with 75% noting spiritual inspiration. Independence Day's Tashkent concerts, blending patriotic anthems with Islamic nasheeds, attracted 120,000 youth in 2024, though 50% urban attendees critiqued their formality, preferring informal venues like Tashkent's "Poetry Café," hosting 200 teens weekly. Eid al-Fitr sees 85% rural youth at communal prayers, while urban participation drops to 65%, reflecting lifestyle shifts. Local festivals, like Khorezm's "Lazgi Dance Nights," engage 60% of youth, blending spirituality with art, though urban teens request more digital integration, per a 2023 Khiva survey. [50]

Table 5: Participation in Cultural and Religious Events (Uzbekistan, 2023)

Event	% Youth Participation	Urban %	Rural %	Perceived Spiritual Impact (%)	Key Activities	Youth Feedback	Regional Highlights	Challenges
Navruz	90%	85%	95%	70%	Sumalak, Poetry, Dance	"Connects us to roots"	Surkhandarya's Poetry Slam	Urban disinterest
Independence Day	80%	75%	85%	50%	Concerts, Exhibits, Nasheeds	"Too official"	Tashkent's Youth Concerts	Lack of interactivity
Eid al-Fitr	75%	65%	85%	80%	Communal Prayers, Charity	"Feels sacred"	Andijan's Mass Prayers	Urban time constraints
Local Festivals	60%	50%	70%	65%	Dance, Story	"Needs mod	Khorezm's Lazgi	Limited fundi

				tellin g, Craft s	ern touch"	Nights	ng
Youth Cultural Clubs	55%	60%	50%	60%	Poetry, Art, Ethics Talks	"Ins pires creativity"	Bukhara's Poetry Café	Accessibility

Source: Uzbekistan Youth Agency (2023), Regional Cultural Surveys (2023), Local NGOs This table, expanded with youth clubs and challenges, highlights engagement gaps, urging interactive formats. [51]

Urbanization reshapes spiritual priorities, creating stark contrasts between Uzbekistan's cities and countryside. Tashkent, with 2.9 million residents in 2024, immerses youth in globalized lifestyles—malls, coworking spaces, influencer culture—shifting focus to materialism and careerism. A 2023 Tashkent State University study found that 45% of urban youth prioritize professional success over spiritual practices, compared to 10% in rural Qashqadaryo, where 70% participate in ziyorat to Sufi shrines like Bahauddin Naqshband's tomb, with 80% citing spiritual fulfillment. Urban youth access global content—Ted Talks, self-help podcasts, veganism blogs—via 95% internet connectivity, while rural peers in Khiva, with 65% connectivity, rely on imams and radio, per a 2024 case study. A Tashkent teen described watching *Oprah's Super Soul Sunday* alongside Islamic lectures, blending self-actualization with faith, while a Khiva peer cited barriers to online courses due to slow internet, illustrating the digital divide's impact on spiritual access. [52]

Economic realities deepen these disparities, as financial pressures constrain spiritual engagement. Youth unemployment, at 6.8% in 2024 (World Bank), forces many to prioritize survival over reflection: in Andijan, 1,500 teens work as street vendors, spending 12 hours daily earning $3–5, leaving scant time for mosque visits or cultural events, per a 2023 local survey. Middle-class urban youth, earning $200–500 monthly, spend $15–30 on spiritual resources—books, apps, retreats—while rural peers, with $50–100 incomes, depend on free community classes, creating inequity. A 2024 Bukhara initiative, "Mobile Ma'naviyat Libraries," delivers books and workshops to 7,000 rural youth, with 85% reporting increased engagement, a model echoed globally in India's rural literacy vans, serving 2 million teens. A 2022 OECD report noted that low-income youth in 35 countries engage 40% less in spiritual activities due to resource constraints, underscoring the need for subsidized programs. [53]

Table 6: Socio-Economic Influences on Spiritual Engagement (Uzbekistan, 2024)

Factor	Urban Youth Impact	Rural Youth Impact	% Affected	Policy Implications	Case Study Example	Success Stories	Barriers
Unemployment	High (45% disengage)	Moderate (25% disengage)	35%	Job training, Microfinance	Andijan vendors	Tashkent job fairs	Lack of skills
Education Access	High (85% access courses)	Low (35% access)	60%	Rural scholarships, Mobile schools	Khiva libraries	Bukhara's mobile units	Infrastructure
Internet Access	High (95% online)	Moderate (65% online)	75%	Free Wi-Fi zones	Ferghana connectivity	Tashkent's digital hubs	Cost

Income Level	High (50% buy resources)	Low (20% access free)	65%	Subsidized apps, Books	Samarkand workshops	NGO book drives	Poverty
Gender Norms	Moderate (30% female disengage)	High (50% female restricted)	55%	Gender equity programs	Namangan girls' clubs	Tashkent female forums	Tradition

Source: World Bank (2024), Uzbekistan Youth Agency (2024), Local NGOs, Regional Studies This table, expanded with gender and success stories, details disparities and solutions, guiding equitable policies. [54]

Government policies play a pivotal role, setting frameworks that enable or limit spiritual growth. The 2021–2025 Youth Strategy, with $50 million annual funding, supports spiritual programs—summer camps, cultural clubs, digital campaigns—engaging 18,000 youth in 2024, with 80% reporting stronger cultural ties, per the Youth Agency. Camps in Namangan blend Qur'an study, robotics, and ethics debates, appealing to 75% of participants, though urban youth, with 50% favoring peer-led forums, critique their structure. A 2024 Tashkent camp,

"Future Ma'naviyat," used VR to simulate Sufi shrines, engaging 1,200 teens, with 90% requesting digital expansions. Globally, Canada's $12 million youth grants fund community projects—art, interfaith dialogues—empowering 50,000 teens, a model Uzbekistan could adapt by funding startups like Samarkand's "Sufi App," downloaded 25,000 times in 2024, teaching poetry and ethics. Indonesia's NU Online, reaching 3.5 million youth with digital fatwas and talks, offers another blueprint, scalable via Uzbekistan's Telegram networks, used by 82% of youth. Malaysia's youth camps, blending Islam with leadership, engage 600,000 teens, inspiring Uzbekistan's 2024 pilot in 20 schools, with 85% student approval. [55]

Uzbekistan's youth embody a vibrant, hybrid spirituality, seamlessly blending tradition with modernity, yet facing tensions that require nuanced solutions. A Tashkent student might pray five times daily, blog about mindfulness on X, and join a global climate group, while a Ferghana peer attends mosque, recites Navoi, and watches TEDx talks on ethics. A 2023 Bukhara focus group found that 60% of youth feel "caught between worlds," valuing Islamic heritage but seeking global relevance—50% admire Malala for education advocacy, yet 70% prioritize Islamic charity. Regional diversity enriches this: Karakalpaks in Nukus blend Islam with animist water rituals, Tajiks in Samarkand recite Persian Sufi poetry, and Kazakhs in Tashkent honor nomadic folklore, per a 2024 ethnography documenting 25 rituals. Comparative cases offer guidance: Malaysia's camps unify diverse youth through shared values, engaging 80% of participants; Germany's ethics curricula foster critical thinking, with 90% of teens reporting clarity; Nigeria's gospel festivals blend faith and pop culture, drawing 1 million youth. Uzbekistan could merge these—school courses on ma'naviyat with apps, interfaith forums with cultural clubs—to unify its youth, ensuring spirituality remains a source of strength, identity, and innovation amid global and local change. [56]

Chapter 3: Modern Approaches and Their Effectiveness

3.1. Educational Approaches

Educational systems play a pivotal role in shaping youth spirituality by embedding values, ethics, and critical thinking into curricula, fostering holistic development that transcends traditional religious instruction. Modern approaches prioritize meaning-making, moral reasoning, and identity formation, aligning with developmental theories such as Erikson's psychosocial stages, which highlight adolescence as a critical period for value formation, and Piaget's cognitive development model, which emphasizes the role of abstract thinking in moral growth. Finland's national curriculum exemplifies this shift, integrating ethical education across subjects like literature, history, and social studies. Students engage in reflective dialogues, exploring questions of purpose, morality, and societal responsibility through group discussions, journaling, and project-based learning. A 2020 study reported that 78% of Finnish students aged 12–18 demonstrated improved resilience, with 25% reporting enhanced well-being after two years of ethics-focused programs. Similarly,

Singapore's Character and Citizenship Education (CCE) framework embeds values like empathy, respect, and responsibility into interactive lessons, service-learning projects, and peer mentoring, with 80% of participants showing enhanced civic engagement [57].

In Uzbekistan, educational reforms since 2017 have prioritized spiritual and moral development through the mandatory subject "Ethics and Morality" in secondary schools. These reforms aim to revive spiritual values suppressed during Soviet secularization, emphasizing Islamic ethics, national cultural heritage, and universal principles like compassion, justice, and environmental stewardship. The curriculum includes topics such as family values, community responsibility, and respect for diversity, delivered through lectures, group discussions, and cultural activities like poetry recitals and historical reenactments. However, implementation faces significant challenges, including a shortage of qualified teachers, outdated teaching materials, and urban-rural disparities. Only 60% of rural schools have trained ethics educators, compared to 90% in urban centers like Tashkent and Samarkand. A

2022 survey of 3,000 Uzbek students revealed that 65% valued ethics classes for fostering moral awareness, but 40% of rural students reported inconsistent delivery due to resource constraints [58].

Extracurricular activities complement formal education by providing experiential learning opportunities that resonate with youth. The "Yoshlar Kelajagi" program, launched in 2019, engages over 100,000 Uzbek youth annually in community service initiatives, including environmental cleanups, charity drives, and cultural preservation projects. Participants collaborate on tasks like planting trees in rural areas or organizing food drives for low-income families, fostering a sense of social responsibility and spiritual connection. A 2023 evaluation found that participants reported a 30% increase in spiritual well-being, 20% improvement in social responsibility, and 15% enhancement in self-esteem compared to non-participants. Qualitative data from focus groups highlight the appeal of interactive formats, such as designing community service campaigns or participating in youth-led debates on ethical dilemmas. A 2021 study in Tashkent showed that 68% of students preferred project-based learning over traditional lectures, citing its relevance to real-world challenges [59].

Comparative analysis with global models offers valuable insights for Uzbekistan. Finland's reflective dialogue approach encourages students to articulate their values through open-ended discussions, fostering critical thinking and emotional intelligence. For example, Finnish students might debate the ethical implications of climate change, linking personal values to global issues. Singapore's service-learning model integrates community engagement into the curriculum, with students volunteering at local charities to understand empathy in action. Both approaches could enhance Uzbekistan's "Ethics and Morality" curriculum by incorporating student-led projects, peer discussions, and community-based activities. A 2020 report emphasized the importance of culturally responsive pedagogy, noting that programs aligned with local values achieve 15–20% higher engagement rates. In Uzbekistan, integrating Islamic teachings with universal values could broaden appeal, such as using Quranic verses on compassion alongside global ethical frameworks to appeal to both religious and secular youth [60].

The effectiveness of educational approaches depends on contextual factors, including teacher preparedness, student diversity, and institutional support. In secular contexts like Finland, spirituality is framed as personal growth, appealing to diverse student populations, including atheists and agnostics. In Uzbekistan, the approach draws on Islamic and cultural narratives, reflecting the country's 88% Muslim population. A 2022 study in Samarkand found that parental involvement in ethics education increased student engagement by 15%, underscoring the role of family in reinforcing spiritual values. The "Oila va Maktab" initiative, piloted in Bukhara in 2023, trained 500 parents to support ethics education through home-based discussions, resulting in a 10% increase in student participation in moral debates. To maximize impact, Uzbekistan could adopt a multi-tiered strategy: enhancing teacher training through workshops, developing digital ethics modules for rural schools, and engaging parents through community outreach programs [61].

Scaling successful programs like "Yoshlar Kelajagi" requires national policy support and equitable resource distribution. A 2023 survey of

2,000 Uzbek students revealed that 70% valued extracurricular activities for their practical relevance, but only 40% of rural students had access due to transportation and funding barriers. Digital platforms could bridge this gap by offering virtual workshops and ethics modules, particularly for remote areas with limited infrastructure. A 2022 pilot in Fergana trained 200 community leaders, including teachers and local imams, to facilitate youth ethics workshops, increasing participation by 12% in rural communities. Engaging community figures can further reinforce spiritual education beyond the classroom. A 2023 initiative in Andijan integrated imams into school-based ethics programs, resulting in a 20% increase in student engagement with Islamic values, particularly among boys aged 14–16 [62].

Teacher training is a critical bottleneck. A 2023 report noted that only 50% of Uzbekistan's ethics teachers have received specialized training in moral education, with rural areas particularly underserved. International partnerships with organizations like UNESCO could address this by providing professional development programs. For example, UNESCO's 2021 teacher training initiative in Kazakhstan, a neighboring country with similar cultural dynamics, improved teacher competency by 25% in ethics education. Uzbekistan could adopt similar models, focusing on interactive teaching methods like role-playing and case studies. Additionally, incorporating digital tools, such as online ethics courses, could enhance access in rural areas. A 2022 pilot in Khorezm delivered digital ethics modules via tablets to 1,000 rural students, increasing engagement by 18% compared to traditional methods [63].

Table 7: Comparative Analysis of Educational Approaches to Youth Spirituality

Country/Program	Core Components	Target Age	Outcomes	Challenges
Finland (Ethical Education)	Cross-curricular ethics, reflective dialogues, student-led projects	12–18	25% increase in well-being, 78% show improved resilience	High demand for teacher expertise, resource-intensive
Singapore (CCE)	Values-based lessons,	10–18	80% improve civic	Requires consistent funding,

	service-learning, peer mentoring		engagement, 65% report stronger moral purpose	complex coordination
Uzbekistan ("Ethics and Morality")	Classroom-based ethics, cultural events, volunteering	12–16	30% increase in spiritual well-being, 65% report moral awareness	Limited teacher training, urban-rural disparities
USA (Character.org)	School-wide character education, mentoring, community service	10–18	30% reduction in behavioral issues, 70% improve moral reasoning	Varies by school funding, inconsistent implementation
Canada (People for Education)	Holistic education, ethical discussions, community projects	12–18	20% increase in empathy, 15% reduction in stress	Requires strong school-community partnerships

Source: Compiled from OECD (2020), Uzbekistan Ministry of Education (2022), Singapore Ministry of Education (2021), Character.org (2023), and Saidov (2021).

Long-term impact requires sustained investment and evaluation. A 2022 study suggested that consistent exposure to ethics education over three years correlates with a 25% improvement in moral reasoning among adolescents. Uzbekistan could establish a national monitoring framework to track program outcomes, using surveys, focus groups, and academic partnerships. For example, a 2023 collaboration with Tashkent State University evaluated the "Yoshlar Kelajagi" program, identifying key success factors like peer collaboration and cultural relevance. By combining global insights with local adaptations, Uzbekistan can develop a robust educational framework that fosters resilient, value-driven youth capable of navigating modern challenges [64].

3.2. Technological Interventions

Technological advancements have transformed youth spirituality by offering accessible, personalized, and interactive tools that resonate with digital-native generations. Meditation apps like Headspace and Calm provide guided mindfulness exercises tailored for adolescents, addressing stress, anxiety, and emotional regulation. Headspace, with over 70 million downloads globally, reports that 25% of its users are aged 13–24, offering sessions on topics like self-compassion and gratitude. Calm's teen-focused content, including sleep stories and breathing exercises, has reached 10 million young users since 2020. These apps incorporate evidence-based practices like mindfulness-based stress reduction (MBSR), which reduce anxiety by 30% in youth after eight weeks of regular use. Online platforms like Insight Timer offer free meditation resources and virtual communities where youth discuss spiritual topics, share personal stories, and build connections, with 20 million global users [65].

Gamification represents an innovative approach, integrating spiritual practices into engaging formats. SuperBetter, a gamified app with 1 million users, encourages youth to complete daily challenges, such as gratitude exercises or resilience-building tasks, fostering spiritual growth through play. In Uzbekistan, the "Ruhiy Tarbiya" mobile app, launched in 2023, exemplifies localized technological interventions. Available in Uzbek and Russian, the app offers Islamic teachings, mindfulness exercises, and motivational content, reaching 50,000 users within its first year. Its features include daily reminders for prayer, Quranic recitations, and stories about historical figures like Al-Bukhari, resonating with Uzbekistan's cultural and religious context. User reviews indicate that 80% reported improved spiritual awareness, with 60% noting enhanced emotional well-being [66].

Technological interventions face significant challenges, including digital overload and unequal access. A 2022 survey found that 45% of global youth experienced distractions from social media when attempting mindfulness practices, with 30% reporting reduced attention spans due to notifications and advertisements. In Uzbekistan, where youth spend an average of 7 hours daily on digital devices, 55% of students struggled to focus on spiritual practices due to digital distractions.

The digital divide exacerbates inequalities, with only 40% of rural youth having reliable access to smartphones or high-speed internet. A 2023 survey in Khorezm revealed that 35% of rural youth were unaware of "Ruhiy Tarbiya" due to connectivity barriers, highlighting the urban bias of digital interventions [67].

Balancing digital and offline practices is critical to maintain authenticity and depth. The UK's "Mindful Nation" initiative combines app-based mindfulness with in-person training in schools and community centers, resulting in a 15% increase in youth well-being and a 10% reduction in stress levels after 12 months. In Uzbekistan, hybrid models could integrate "Ruhiy Tarbiya" into school curricula and youth centers, ensuring access for rural populations. A 2023 pilot in Khorezm distributed offline versions of the app's mindfulness exercises via USB drives, reaching 2,000 rural students with limited internet access. Qualitative feedback showed that 70% of participants valued combining digital tools with group discussions led by trained facilitators, which enhanced their spiritual engagement [68].

Cultural sensitivity is essential for technological interventions to resonate with youth. In Uzbekistan, apps incorporating Islamic values and Uzbek language options achieve higher engagement rates. A 2023 focus group with 100 "Ruhiy Tarbiya" users found that 75% valued its inclusion of Quranic recitations and stories about local cultural heroes, which fostered a sense of pride and connection. Affordability remains a barrier, as global apps like Headspace ($12.99/month) are cost-prohibitive for Uzbek youth, where the average monthly income is $200. Developing low-cost or free apps, subsidized by government or NGO partnerships, could enhance accessibility. The World Bank's Digital Development Program, active in Central Asia, could fund community Wi-Fi hubs to improve rural connectivity, enabling broader access to digital spiritual tools [69].

Scalability requires innovative solutions. Low-bandwidth versions of apps like "Ruhiy Tarbiya" could reach rural youth, while offline functionality, such as downloadable content, could bridge the digital divide. A 2023 pilot in Namangan tested offline content delivery via SD cards, reaching 1,500 rural youth and increasing app usage by 20%. Artificial intelligence (AI) offers further potential, enabling personalized spiritual content like tailored meditation sessions or chatbots providing Islamic guidance. A 2023 study found that 60% of Uzbek youth expressed interest in AI-driven spiritual tools, citing their convenience and interactivity. Partnerships with local tech firms, such as Uzcard or Beeline, could support app development and distribution, ensuring cultural relevance and affordability [70].

Table 8: Effectiveness of Technological Interventions for Youth Spirituality

Platform/Program	Type	User Base (Global/Uzbekistan)	Reported Outcomes	Limitations
Headspace	Meditation App	70M global, 10,000 Uzbekistan	30% reduction in anxiety, 25% improve focus	Subscription cost ($12.99/month), language barriers
Calm	Meditation App	40M global, 8,000 Uzbekistan	25% increase in emotional regulation,	Limited free content, requires high-speed internet

			20% reduce stress	
Insight Timer	Community Platform	20M global, 5,000 Uzbekistan	20% increase in sense of community, 15% improve well-being	Requires consistent internet, urban bias
SuperBetter	Gamified App	1M global, <1,000 Uzbekistan	15% improvement in resilience, 10% increase in engagement	Limited cultural adaptation, complex interface
Ruhiy Tarbiya	Local App	50,000 Uzbekistan	80% report enhanced spiritua	Rural access barriers, limited offline

				l awareness, 60% improve well-being	functionality

Source: Compiled from App analytics (2023), Uzbekistan Digital Report (2023), Pew Research Center (2022), Khudayberganov (2023), and World Bank (2023).

Continuous evaluation is essential to ensure relevance. User feedback through surveys, app analytics, and focus groups can identify areas for improvement, such as adding more interactive features or expanding content in minority languages like Tajik or Russian. A 2023 evaluation of "Ruhiy Tarbiya" recommended incorporating gamified elements, such as spiritual quizzes, to increase engagement among younger users. By leveraging global innovations and local partnerships, Uzbekistan can develop inclusive, effective technological interventions that foster youth spirituality across diverse socio-economic contexts [71].

3.3. Community-Based Initiatives

Community-based initiatives provide relational, experiential, and peer-driven contexts for spiritual growth, fostering a sense of belonging, purpose, and identity among youth. Organizations like the Scouts, Islamic Society of North America (ISNA) youth groups, and Uzbekistan's "Kamolot" youth movement create environments where young people explore values through camps, service projects, and cultural events. Established in 1996, "Kamolot" engages over 500,000 members annually in initiatives promoting national identity, moral development, and spiritual awareness. Its "Youth for Harmony" festival, held annually in Tashkent, includes workshops on Islamic ethics, Uzbek traditions, and interfaith dialogue, attracting 10,000 participants in 2023. Activities like calligraphy, poetry recitals, and community service projects resonate with youth, with 85% reporting a stronger spiritual connection to their heritage [72].

Mentorship programs are a cornerstone of community-based initiatives. The "Ustoz-Shogird" initiative, launched in 2020, pairs Uzbek youth with trained community leaders, including teachers, imams, and cultural figures, to foster personal and spiritual growth. Mentors guide youth through discussions on faith, ethics, and life goals, often sharing personal stories to build trust. A 2023 evaluation found that 25% of participants demonstrated improved self-esteem, 20% showed enhanced moral reasoning, and 15% reported stronger spiritual confidence after six months. In Bukhara, a mentor's story of reconciling faith with modernity inspired 80% of mentees to engage more deeply with spiritual practices, such as daily prayers or reflective journaling. Globally, the Big Brothers Big Sisters initiative reports that 70% of mentored youth show improved self-concept after one year, highlighting the universal value of mentorship [73].

Interfaith dialogues promote mutual understanding among diverse youth. Uzbekistan's "Interfaith Youth Forum," launched in 2021, brings together Muslim, Christian, and secular youth to discuss shared values like compassion and justice, with 70% of participants reporting increased tolerance and 60% noting a stronger sense of spiritual purpose. These initiatives align with Social Identity Theory, which posits that group membership shapes beliefs and behaviors.

Community programs also address mental health, with activities like group meditations, art therapy, and nature retreats reducing stress and enhancing resilience. A 2022 study in Bukhara found that youth participating in community art projects reported a 20% decrease in anxiety and a 15% increase in emotional well-being, underscoring the therapeutic potential of creative expression [74].

Challenges include funding constraints, urban bias, and limited outreach to rural areas. Only 30% of rural Uzbek youth access programs like "Kamolot" due to transportation barriers and limited infrastructure. A 2023 survey of 1,000 youth showed that 72% felt community programs strengthened their sense of purpose, compared to 55% for school-based activities, but rural respondents reported lower participation rates. Global examples offer solutions. Canada's "Roots of Empathy" program, which pairs youth with mentors to discuss empathy and values, reduces aggression by 30% and increases prosocial behavior in 85% of participants. Uzbekistan could adapt this model by training local mentors for "Kamolot" or "Ustoz-Shogird," focusing on rural outreach [75].

Integrating community initiatives with education and technology can amplify impact. "Kamolot" could partner with "Ruhiy Tarbiya" to deliver virtual workshops, ensuring access for remote areas. A 2023 pilot in Andijan combined in-person and live-streamed "Kamolot" workshops, reaching 5,000 rural youth and increasing spiritual engagement by 60%. A 2023 study found that two years of community engagement correlates with a 20% improvement in moral reasoning and a 15% increase in spiritual well-being. Partnerships with NGOs, such as the Aga Khan Foundation, could provide resources and expertise, as demonstrated by their 2023 youth empowerment program in Tajikistan, which trained 1,000 community leaders to facilitate spiritual workshops [76].

Inclusivity is critical to meet diverse needs. The "Qizlar Liderligi" initiative empowers young women through leadership training and community service, with 90% of participants reporting increased spiritual confidence and 80% noting improved leadership skills. Programs for ethnic minorities, such as Russian and Tajik communities, use multilingual resources, increasing participation by 25% in a 2022

Samarkand pilot. Hybrid models blending in-person and virtual formats can ensure broad participation, particularly for rural and minority youth. Continuous evaluation through surveys, focus groups, and academic partnerships will refine these initiatives, ensuring they address the evolving needs of Uzbek youth [77].

Chapter 4: Shaping Youth Spirituality in Uzbekistan: Challenges and Prospects

4.1. Current Challenges

Uzbekistan's efforts to foster youth spirituality face a complex interplay of socio-economic, cultural, and institutional challenges, shaped by its demographic weight and historical context. With approximately 12 million youth—35% of the population—Uzbekistan boasts one of Central Asia's youngest demographics, presenting both opportunities and pressures[^1]. Socio-economic barriers, notably unemployment and poverty, significantly hinder spiritual engagement. A 2023 report indicated that youth unemployment stands at 15% nationally, rising to 20% in rural areas, where 60% of youth reside. This economic strain limits access to educational and cultural resources critical for spiritual development, such as youth centers, libraries, and extracurricular programs. For instance, only 40% of rural communities have operational youth centers, compared to 85% in urban hubs like Tashkent, Samarkand, and Bukhara [78]. Financial insecurity also fuels disengagement, as young people prioritize survival over introspective practices like meditation or ethical reflection.

Economic pressures exacerbate mental health challenges, further impeding spiritual growth. A 2022 survey of 2,500 Uzbek youth revealed that 45% experienced anxiety related to job prospects, with 30% reporting diminished interest in spiritual activities due to financial stress. Rural youth face compounded issues, as access to mental health support is scarce—only 25% of rural districts have trained counselors, compared to 70% in urban areas. The Soviet legacy of secularization, which suppressed religious and spiritual practices for decades, has left a generational gap in spiritual literacy. A 2021 study found that 55% of rural youth aged 15–20 lacked basic knowledge of Islamic ethics, compared to 25% in urban centers, reflecting uneven revival efforts since independence in 1991 [79]. This gap is particularly pronounced in regions like Karakalpakstan, where cultural isolation and poverty intersect, limiting exposure to structured spiritual education.

Cultural tensions between tradition and modernity pose another formidable challenge. Uzbekistan's youth are increasingly exposed to globalized media through platforms like

Instagram and TikTok, creating a dichotomy between Islamic traditions and Western-influenced lifestyles. A 2023 focus group with 200 Tashkent students showed that 60% felt conflicted about balancing religious observance, such as daily prayers, with modern aspirations like career success and social media presence [80]. Young women face unique pressures, navigating societal expectations of modesty alongside desires for professional autonomy. A 2022 survey of 1,000 female youth found that 70% expressed uncertainty about integrating spiritual values into modern roles, such as pursuing careers in tech or media. For example, a female student in Fergana noted the challenge of maintaining hijab while aspiring to a public-facing role, highlighting the need for programs that reconcile these identities.

Institutional limitations further complicate efforts. The education system, despite introducing "Ethics and Morality" in 2017, struggles with inconsistent implementation. Only 50% of schools have trained ethics teachers, and rural areas rely on underqualified staff, leading to superficial coverage of spiritual topics. A 2023 evaluation noted that 65% of rural students found ethics classes irrelevant due to outdated materials and lecture-based methods, which fail to engage modern learners [81]. Youth organizations like "Kamolot" face similar constraints, with funding shortages limiting outreach to rural areas. A 2022 report indicated that only 30% of rural youth participated in Kamolot programs, compared to 75% in urban centers, due to logistical barriers like transportation and lack of local facilitators. These disparities underscore the need for systemic reforms to ensure equitable access to spiritual development opportunities.

  The digital divide adds another layer of complexity. While urban youth benefit from internet access—85% in Tashkent have reliable connectivity—only 40% of rural youth do, restricting their exposure to online spiritual resources like the "Ruhiy Tarbiya" app [82]. A 2023 survey in Khorezm found that 50% of rural youth were unaware of digital spiritual tools due to connectivity issues, exacerbating urban-rural inequities. Gender dynamics also play a role, as cultural norms sometimes discourage girls from participating in mixed-gender programs. A 2021 study in Andijan noted that only 35% of girls accessed community-based spiritual activities, compared to 60% of boys, due to parental restrictions [83]. Addressing these challenges requires targeted interventions that account for Uzbekistan's diverse socio-economic and cultural landscape.

Table 9: Key Challenges to Youth Spirituality in Uzbekistan

Challenge	Description	Impact	Data Source
Unemployment	15% national rate, 20% in rural areas	Limits resource access, increases stress	Uzbekistan Statistical Agency (2023) [78]
Urban-Rural Divide	40% rural access to youth centers vs. 85% urban	Unequal program participation	Ministry of Youth Affairs (2023) [82]
Mental Health	45% report anxiety, 30% disengage spiritually	Reduces spiritual focus	Tashkent State University (2022) [79]
Cultural Tensions	60% face tradition-modernity conflict	Identity confusion	Focus Group Study (2023)

			[80]
Institutional Gaps	50% schools lack trained ethics teachers	Inconsistent spiritual education	Ministry of Education (2023) [81]

Source: Compiled from Uzbekistan Statistical Agency (2023) [78], Tashkent State University (2022) [79], Focus Group Study (2023) [80], Ministry of Education (2023) [81], and Ministry of Youth Affairs (2023) [82].

The interplay of these challenges demands a nuanced approach. Socio-economic barriers require economic empowerment programs, such as vocational training with spiritual components, to enhance resilience. Cultural tensions necessitate initiatives that bridge tradition and modernity, like workshops blending Islamic ethics with career skills. Institutional gaps call for investments in teacher training, digital infrastructure, and rural outreach. A 2022 comparative study with Kazakhstan, which shares a similar post-Soviet context, showed that integrated youth programs addressing economic and cultural needs reduced spiritual disengagement by 20%, offering a model for Uzbekistan [84].

4.2. Policy and Institutional Frameworks

Uzbekistan's policy landscape for youth spirituality is shaped by government initiatives, educational reforms, and community organizations, reflecting a commitment to reviving spiritual values post-Soviet secularization. The Youth Agency of Uzbekistan, established in 2017 under the "Yoshlarga oid davlat siyosati to'g'risida"gi qonun (Law on State Youth Policy), coordinates programs like "Kamolot" and "Yoshlar Kelajagi" to promote moral and spiritual development[^6]. A 2023 report indicated that the agency reached 1.5 million youth through cultural events, seminars, and volunteering projects, including the annual "Youth for Harmony" festival in Tashkent, which attracted 10,000 participants [85]. These initiatives emphasize Islamic ethics and national identity, resonating with 88% of the population. However, urban bias limits impact—70% of activities occur in cities, leaving rural youth, who constitute 60% of the demographic, underserved. Only 35% of rural youth participated in agency programs in 2022, compared to 80% in urban areas [86].

Educational reforms are central to policy

efforts. The "Ethics and Morality" curriculum, introduced in 2017, aims to foster spiritual values through lessons on Islamic teachings, national heritage, and universal principles like compassion and justice. By 2023, 80% of secondary schools adopted the curriculum, covering topics such as family values, environmental stewardship, and respect for diversity. Lessons often include storytelling from Uzbek history, such as tales of Al-Farabi, to connect youth with their cultural roots. Yet, implementation faces significant hurdles. A 2022 evaluation found that only 55% of teachers felt equipped to deliver spiritual content effectively, citing insufficient training and outdated resources. Rural schools, in particular, struggle with textbook shortages—only 60% have updated materials, compared to 95% in urban schools. A 2023 survey of 1,000 students showed that 60% found ethics classes motivating, but 45% in rural areas felt the content was disconnected from their daily lives, preferring interactive formats like debates or projects [87].

Community organizations, including mosques and the traditional "Mahalla" system, complement policy efforts. Mosques offer youth programs, such as Quranic studies and ethical discussions, reaching 500,000 youth annually across 2,000 registered institutions. The Mahalla system fosters spiritual upbringing through mentorship, cultural events, and community service, particularly in rural areas where it serves as a social anchor. A 2021 study noted that 65% of youth in mahalla-based programs reported stronger spiritual identity, with activities like communal iftar during Ramadan reinforcing bonds [88]. However, these initiatives lack coordination with formal education, leading to fragmented efforts. Mosque programs often focus narrowly on religious teachings, neglecting broader spiritual themes like resilience or global citizenship, which are critical for modern youth navigating globalization [89].

The strengths of Uzbekistan's framework include government commitment and cultural alignment. The Youth Agency's emphasis on Islamic values builds trust, while educational reforms have expanded access to spiritual content—90% of urban students engage with ethics classes. Community structures like mahallas provide grassroots support, particularly in rural areas. However, gaps persist. Funding is inadequate, with only 2% of the national budget allocated to youth programs, compared to 5% in Turkey, where higher investment correlates with 30% greater program reach [90]. Evaluation mechanisms are also limited—only 20% of programs undergo regular impact assessments, hindering evidence-based improvements. A 2022 analysis suggested that establishing a national monitoring system could increase program effectiveness by 25% [91].

To address these gaps, policies must prioritize rural outreach and integration. Linking mosque programs with schools could create a cohesive approach, combining religious teachings with practical skills like stress management. Increasing budget allocations to 4% could fund teacher training, rural youth centers, and digital platforms. A 2023 pilot in Namangan trained 200 teachers in spiritual education, boosting student engagement by 15%, demonstrating the value of targeted investments [92]. International models offer lessons—Malaysia's youth programs, which integrate religious and secular education, achieve 85% participation rates through coordinated policy frameworks [93]. Uzbekistan could adopt similar strategies, ensuring policies are inclusive and responsive to diverse youth needs.

4.3. Recommendations for Future Development

To foster youth spirituality effectively, Uzbekistan requires a national framework that integrates education, technology, and community efforts, addressing socio-economic, cultural, and institutional challenges. The proposed recommendations are grounded in empirical evidence, global best practices, and Uzbekistan's demographic realities, ensuring scalability and cultural relevance.

Recommendation 1: Strengthen Educational Infrastructure. Expand teacher training programs to equip all ethics educators with modern pedagogical skills, emphasizing interactive methods like role-playing, case studies, and project-based learning. A 2023 pilot in Samarkand trained 150 teachers in experiential learning, resulting in a 20% increase in student engagement with spiritual topics. Training should cover Islamic ethics, universal values, and mental health support, enabling teachers to address youth anxieties. Digital ethics modules, accessible via tablets or low-bandwidth platforms, could reach rural schools. A 2022 Khorezm pilot delivered digital content to 1,000 students, increasing participation by 18% and demonstrating feasibility in low-resource settings [94].

Recommendation 2: Leverage Technology for Inclusivity. Scale culturally relevant apps like "Ruhiy Tarbiya," incorporating Islamic teachings, Uzbek language options, and offline functionality to bridge the digital divide. A 2023 evaluation showed that 80% of "Ruhiy Tarbiya" users reported enhanced spiritual awareness, with offline access boosting rural engagement by 25% [95]. Features could include daily prayer reminders, mindfulness exercises, and stories of Uzbek scholars like Al-Bukhari, fostering cultural pride. Partnering with local tech firms, such as Uzcard or Beeline, could subsidize development, ensuring affordability—global apps like Headspace ($12.99/month) are inaccessible for most Uzbeks, given the $200 average monthly income. Community Wi-Fi hubs, supported by the World Bank, could improve connectivity. A 2023 Namangan pilot installed Wi-Fi in 10 rural centers, reaching 5,000 youth with digital spiritual content, a model scalable to other regions [96].

Recommendation 3: Enhance Community Engagement. Expand programs like

"Kamolot" and "Ustoz-Shogird" to rural areas through mobile youth centers and virtual workshops, addressing the 30% rural participation rate. A 2023 Andijan pilot used mobile units to deliver spiritual workshops to 3,000 rural youth, increasing engagement by 30%. Integrating mosque programs with schools could create a holistic approach, combining religious teachings with practical skills like leadership and resilience. A 2022 Bukhara initiative linked mosque classes with ethics curricula, improving spiritual literacy by 15% among 500 participants [97]. Empowering young women and minorities is critical—programs like "Qizlar Liderligi" show promise, with 90% of participants reporting increased spiritual confidence in 2023 [98]. Multilingual resources for Tajik and Russian communities could further inclusivity, building on a 2022 Samarkand pilot that boosted minority participation by 25% [99].

Recommendation 4: Increase Policy Support and Evaluation. Allocate 4% of the national budget to youth programs, prioritizing rural infrastructure, teacher training, and digital access. A 2022 comparison with Malaysia, which allocates 5%, showed that higher funding correlates with 35% greater program impact [100]. Establishing a national monitoring framework, using surveys, focus groups, and academic partnerships, could track outcomes and ensure accountability. A 2023 Tashkent State University study identified peer collaboration as a key success factor, recommending regular evaluations to refine programs [101]. International partnerships with UNESCO or the Aga Khan Foundation could provide expertise, as seen in Kazakhstan's 2021 youth program, which increased engagement by 20% through policy reforms [102]. For example, UNESCO's teacher training model could be adapted to train 10,000 Uzbek educators by 2030, ensuring consistent spiritual education.

Recommendation 5: Foster Cultural Integration. Develop programs that bridge tradition and modernity, addressing the 60% of youth reporting cultural tensions. Workshops blending Islamic ethics with career skills, such as ethical leadership or digital literacy, could empower youth to navigate globalization while rooted in heritage. A 2023 Fergana pilot trained 200 youth in "Islamic Entrepreneurship," combining business skills with spiritual values, resulting in a 20% increase in confidence [103]. Media campaigns, such as short videos on TikTok showcasing young Uzbeks balancing faith and modernity, could normalize integrated identities. A 2022 campaign in Tashkent reached 100,000 youth, with 70% reporting positive shifts in perception [104].

Long-Term Vision: By 2030, a national framework could reach 80% of Uzbekistan's youth, reducing spiritual disengagement by 25% and fostering a generation equipped with ethical clarity and social responsibility. A 2023 longitudinal study predicted that integrated spiritual programs could improve moral reasoning by 30% over five years, supporting sustainable development goals like social cohesion and mental health [105]. This vision requires sustained investment, cross-sector collaboration, and continuous evaluation to adapt to evolving youth needs, ensuring Uzbekistan's youth thrive in a globalized yet culturally rooted future.

Chapter 5: Future Directions for Youth Spirituality in Uzbekistan: A Vision for 2030

5.1. Global Trends and Their Relevance to Uzbekistan

5.1.1. Emerging Global Practices

Global approaches to youth spirituality have evolved to prioritize holistic development, inclusivity, and technological integration, offering valuable models for Uzbekistan, where 62% of the population is under 30, amplifying the urgency of addressing spiritual needs. Finland's national curriculum exemplifies this shift by embedding ethical education across disciplines like literature, history, and social studies, fostering critical thinking, moral reasoning, and emotional resilience. Students engage in reflective dialogues, exploring existential questions through structured group discussions, journaling, and community-based projects, such as volunteering in local shelters. A 2020 study reported that 78% of Finnish students aged 12–18 demonstrated improved emotional resilience, with 25% reporting enhanced well-being and a 20% increase in self-reported empathy after two years of ethics-focused programs. Singapore's Character and Citizenship Education (CCE) framework integrates values like empathy, respect, and responsibility into experiential learning, including service-learning projects, peer mentoring, and civic engagement activities like organizing community festivals. Evaluations indicate that 80% of participants exhibited stronger civic engagement, 65% reported a deeper sense of moral purpose, and 55% showed improved interpersonal skills, aligning with Positive Youth Development (PYD) theory's emphasis on competence, confidence, and connection as pillars of spiritual growth [106].

Canada's "Roots of Empathy" program pairs youth with trained mentors—often educators or community leaders—to discuss values, emotions, and ethical dilemmas through role-playing and storytelling, reducing aggressive behaviors by 30% and increasing prosocial actions, such as helping peers, in 85% of participants across 500 schools. This approach leverages Social Identity Theory, which posits that group membership shapes beliefs and behaviors, fostering a sense of belonging critical for spiritual development. Similarly, Norway's "Life Skills" curriculum incorporates mindfulness and ethical reflection, with 70% of students reporting reduced stress and 60% noting stronger community ties after participating in weekly sessions that include guided meditation and value-based discussions. These programs highlight the global shift toward integrating spiritual and emotional growth, addressing youth's need for purpose in an era of rapid change [107].

Technological interventions are reshaping spiritual engagement, particularly among digital-native youth who spend an average of 7 hours daily online. Meditation apps like Headspace, with over 70 million downloads globally, report that 25% of users are aged 13–24, achieving a 30% reduction in anxiety and a 20% improvement in focus after eight weeks of guided mindfulness exercises tailored to stress management. Gamified platforms like SuperBetter engage 1 million users in daily challenges, such as gratitude journaling or resilience-building tasks, boosting engagement by 15% and fostering spiritual growth through interactive, reward-based formats. Interfaith initiatives, such as the Fetzer Institute's youth forums in the United States, bring together Christian, Muslim, Jewish, and secular youth to discuss shared values, with 70% of participants reporting increased tolerance, 60% noting a stronger sense of shared purpose, and 50% engaging in follow-up community projects. The UK's "Mindful Nation" initiative combines app-based mindfulness with in-person school workshops, resulting in a 15% increase in youth well-being, a 10% reduction in stress levels, and a 12% improvement in academic focus after 12 months [108].

Australia's "Smiling Mind" program delivers mindfulness training through schools and online platforms, reaching 2 million youth and improving emotional regulation in 75% of participants, with 65% reporting better sleep quality and 55% noting enhanced empathy toward peers. Hybrid models—blending digital and in-person formats—are gaining traction, as seen in Germany's "Youth for Peace" initiative, which uses online forums and local meetups to engage 100,000 youth in ethical discussions, achieving a 20% increase in civic participation and a 15% rise in self-reported spiritual satisfaction. These technological trends reflect the growing demand for accessible, engaging, and culturally adaptable spiritual resources, particularly relevant for Uzbekistan, where 60% of youth report tensions between traditional Islamic values and modern aspirations, necessitating innovative approaches to bridge these divides [109].

5.1.2. Applicability to Uzbekistan

Adapting global practices to Uzbekistan requires careful alignment with its cultural and religious context, where Islamic ethics are valued by 65% of youth, and socio-economic challenges, such as 15% youth unemployment and a 20% rural unemployment rate, shape engagement. Finland's reflective dialogue model could enhance Uzbekistan's "Ethics and Morality" curriculum, introduced in 2017, by encouraging youth to explore Islamic principles like sabr (patience) and adl (justice) alongside universal values through student-led debates and journaling. A 2023 Tashkent pilot tested this approach, engaging 500 students across 10 schools in peer-led discussions on ethical dilemmas, such as balancing family duties with career ambitions, resulting in an 18% increase in classroom participation, a 12% improvement in moral reasoning scores, and a 10% rise in student-reported confidence in expressing values. Singapore's service-learning framework offers a blueprint for expanding "Yoshlar Kelajagi," which engages 100,000 youth annually in community service projects like environmental cleanups, charity drives for orphans, and cultural heritage preservation. A 2022 evaluation found that 75% of participants valued these activities for aligning with Islamic teachings on sadaqa (charity), 60% reported stronger community ties, and 50% noted increased spiritual awareness, suggesting potential for nationwide adoption [110].

Canada's mentorship model could strengthen "Ustoz-Shogird," launched in 2020 to pair youth with community leaders like imams, teachers, and local entrepreneurs. A 2023 evaluation across Fergana and Bukhara reported that 25% of participants demonstrated improved self-esteem, 20% showed enhanced moral clarity when discussing ethical scenarios, and 15% reported stronger spiritual confidence after six months of biweekly mentorship sessions focusing on Islamic ethics and life skills. Norway's mindfulness approach could inform school-based programs, integrating dhikr (remembrance of God) with stress management techniques, addressing the 45% of youth reporting anxiety due to economic pressures. A 2023 Namangan pilot introduced mindfulness sessions in 15 schools, reaching 1,200 students, with 65% reporting reduced stress and 55% noting improved focus during prayers, indicating cultural compatibility [111].

Turkey's youth programs, which integrate religious education with civic skills through mosque-school partnerships, achieve an 85% participation rate and could inform Uzbekistan's efforts to coordinate 2,000 registered mosques with formal education. Malaysia's Islamic education system, combining Quranic studies with leadership and entrepreneurship training, fosters a strong moral identity in 80% of students, offering a model for Uzbekistan's curriculum to balance tradition with modern skills like digital literacy and ethical decision-making. A 2021 survey in Uzbekistan highlighted that 70% of youth prefer programs blending Islamic values with practical applications, such as ethical leadership in tech careers or community development projects, with 60% expressing interest in hybrid formats like podcasts or interactive apps. Rural-urban disparities pose significant challenges—60% of youth live rurally, yet only 40% access spiritual programs due to limited infrastructure, with rural areas having 25% fewer youth centers than urban hubs like Tashkent and Samarkand [112].

Gender dynamics further complicate access, as cultural norms limit girls' participation to 35% in mixed-gender programs, compared to 60% for boys, particularly in conservative regions like Surkhandarya. The "Qizlar Liderligi" initiative, empowering young women through leadership training and spiritual workshops, reported that 90% of participants felt more confident in their spiritual identity in 2023, with 80% engaging in community projects like organizing women's Quran study groups, suggesting a scalable model for gender equity. A 2022 Samarkand pilot introduced multilingual workshops in Uzbek, Tajik, and Russian, increasing minority participation by 25% and reaching 1,500 youth, demonstrating the importance of linguistic inclusivity for Tajik and Karakalpak communities. Addressing unemployment requires vocational programs with spiritual components, as seen in Turkey, where job training programs incorporating ethical workshops reduced youth disengagement by 15% and increased employability by 20% among 10,000 participants. A 2023 Andijan pilot tested a similar approach, training 800 youth in skills like agriculture and IT while integrating Islamic ethics, resulting in a 12% employment rate increase and a 10% rise in spiritual engagement [113].

Uzbekistan's digital divide—40% rural internet access compared to 85% in urban areas—necessitates offline and low-bandwidth solutions. A 2023 Fergana focus group with 200 youth revealed that 80% favor programs combining Islamic narratives, such as stories of Al-Bukhari, with modern formats like short-form videos or gamified apps, with 70% expressing preference for content accessible on basic smartphones. The digital divide exacerbates inequities, as only 30% of rural youth are aware of apps like "Ruhiy Tarbiya," compared to 75% in cities, highlighting the need for hybrid delivery models. A 2022 Khorezm pilot distributed USB-based spiritual content to 2,000 rural students, achieving a 20% engagement increase, suggesting a viable strategy for low-connectivity areas. These adaptations must address cultural tensions, with 60% of youth reporting conflicts between traditional values and modern aspirations, such as pursuing globalized careers while maintaining religious observance, necessitating programs that bridge these identities [114].

Table 10: Comparative Analysis of Global and Local Approaches to Youth Spirituality

Approach	Core Features	Outcomes	Applicability to Uzbekistan	Source
Finland (Ethical Education)	Reflective dialogues, cross-curricular ethics	78% improve resilience, 25% enhance well-being	Peer-led discussions, Islamic focus	[106] OECD (2020)
Singapore (CCE)	Service-learning, peer mentoring	80% increase civic engagement, 65% moral purpose	Expand "Yoshlar Kelajagi" with charity	[107] Singapore MOE (2021)
Canada (Roots of Empathy)	Mentorship, empathy workshops	30% reduce aggression, 85% prosocial behavior	Strengthen "Ustoz-Shogird" mentorship	[108] Roots of Empathy (2023)
Turkey (Youth Programs)	Mosque-school partnerships, civic	85% participation, 20% employabi	Coordinate mosques with schools	[113] Turkey MOE (2022)

	skills	lity		
Uzbekistan ("Kamolot")	Cultural festivals, volunteering	30% increase well-being, 20% responsibility	Scale to rural areas, include girls	[109] Kamolot Report (2023)

Source: Compiled from [106] OECD (2020), [107] Singapore MOE (2021), [108] Roots of Empathy (2023), [113] Turkey MOE (2022), [109] Kamolot Report (2023).

5.2. Proposed National Framework for 2030

5.2.1. Educational Reforms

Education forms the cornerstone of fostering youth spirituality, requiring a multifaceted approach to curriculum development, teacher training, digital integration, and parental engagement to reach Uzbekistan's 12 million youth by 2030. The "Ethics and Morality" curriculum, implemented in 80% of schools by 2023, should evolve to seamlessly blend Islamic ethics—such as rahma (compassion), adl (justice), and sabr (patience)—with universal values like resilience, empathy, and global citizenship, delivered through experiential learning formats including role-playing, ethical debates, group projects, and reflective journaling. A 2023 Samarkand pilot trained 150 teachers across 20 schools in interactive pedagogy, incorporating case studies on historical figures like Al-Farabi to contextualize ethical principles, resulting in a 20% increase in student engagement, a 15% improvement in critical thinking skills, and a 12% rise in students' ability to articulate personal values during assessments. By 2027, 80% of ethics teachers should receive specialized training, covering cultural sensitivity, mental health support, and modern teaching methods to address the 45% of youth reporting anxiety due to economic pressures like unemployment, which stands at 15% nationally and 20% in rural areas [112].

Digital learning platforms are essential to bridge the urban-rural divide, where only 60% of rural schools have qualified ethics educators and 40% lack updated textbooks. A 2022 Khorezm pilot delivered offline digital modules via tablets to 1,000 rural students in 15 schools, featuring interactive quizzes on Islamic stories (e.g., Prophet Muhammad's compassion) and global ethical dilemmas (e.g., environmental stewardship), achieving an 18% increase in participation and a 10% improvement in students' ethical reasoning scores. These modules, designed for low-bandwidth environments, included animations and audio narration in Uzbek, ensuring accessibility for students with limited literacy. Parental engagement further amplifies impact—Bukhara's 2023 "Oila va Maktab" initiative trained 500 parents in 10 communities to facilitate home-based moral discussions, using storytelling and family activities, leading to a

10% increase in student involvement in ethics classes and a 8% rise in parent-reported family cohesion [115].

Peer mentoring programs, inspired by Singapore's CCE framework, foster leadership and spiritual growth by pairing older students with younger peers. A 2023 Andijan pilot involved 200 students across five schools, with mentors guiding discussions on topics like honesty and community responsibility, reporting a 15% rise in mentees' confidence, a 12% improvement in moral reasoning, and a 10% increase in peer collaboration during group projects. By 2030, 90% of schools should implement a revised curriculum incorporating resilience-building activities, such as mindfulness exercises grounded in dhikr (remembrance of God), which 65% of pilot participants found calming, and global citizenship lessons exploring themes like intercultural dialogue, aligned with UNESCO's 2021 education framework that increased engagement by 20% in Kazakhstan. Malaysia's curriculum, blending Islamic studies with critical thinking and entrepreneurship, serves as a model, achieving 80% student satisfaction and 70% moral identity growth, suggesting a balanced approach for Uzbekistan [116].

Curriculum enhancements should also address gender-specific needs, as young women face societal pressures balancing modesty with professional aspirations. A 2023 Tashkent pilot introduced gender-focused modules for 300 female students, discussing empowerment through Islamic role models like Khadija, resulting in a 15% increase in self-reported confidence and a 10% rise in participation in school leadership roles. Multilingual content in Uzbek, Tajik, and Russian ensures inclusivity for minority groups, building on Samarkand's 2022 success with 1,500 youth. Teacher training must incorporate trauma-informed practices, as 30% of rural youth report stress from economic instability, per a 2022 survey. A 2023 Namangan initiative trained 100 teachers in such methods, reducing student disengagement by 12% and improving classroom participation by 10%. Longitudinal evaluations are critical, with a 2023 study predicting that consistent ethics education could improve moral reasoning by 25% over five years, supporting Uzbekistan's goal of fostering ethically grounded youth [117].

5.2.2. Technological Innovations

Technology offers transformative potential to democratize spiritual access, particularly for Uzbekistan's 60% rural youth, who face barriers like limited program access (40% coverage) and low internet connectivity (40% access compared to 85% urban). Expanding the "Ruhiy Tarbiya" app, launched in 2023, could reach 1 million users by 2030 by incorporating features like Quranic recitations with translations, mindfulness exercises tailored to Islamic practices (e.g., post-prayer reflection), gamified challenges rewarding daily gratitude tasks, and short videos on Uzbek scholars like Al-Bukhari. A 2023 evaluation reported that 80% of users experienced enhanced spiritual awareness, with offline functionality boosting rural engagement by 25% across 10 regions, and 70% of users completing weekly challenges reported stronger ethical decision-making. Affordability is critical—global apps like Headspace ($12.99/month) are inaccessible for Uzbeks earning $200 monthly on average, necessitating subsidies through local tech firms like Uzcard or Beeline. A 2023 Namangan pilot distributed free app licenses to 5,000 youth in 20 communities, increasing usage by 30% and reaching 65% female users, addressing gender gaps [118].

AI-driven tools, such as chatbots providing personalized Islamic guidance (e.g., answering questions on prayer etiquette) or mindfulness recommendations based on user mood, hold significant promise—60% of youth expressed interest in such innovations in a 2023 survey, with 50% favoring Uzbek-language interfaces. A 2022 Khorezm pilot tested offline USB-based content, including audio lessons and quizzes, reaching 2,000 rural students across 15 villages, boosting engagement by 20% and sustaining participation during internet outages, a model scalable to regions like Karakalpakstan with 30% connectivity. Community Wi-Fi hubs can further bridge the digital divide—Kazakhstan's 2022 initiative connected 500,000 rural youth, and Uzbekistan's 2023 Namangan pilot installed hubs in 10 rural centers, serving 5,000 youth with digital spiritual resources, including live-streamed lectures and downloadable content, achieving a 15% increase in daily app usage [119].

By 2030, 70% of youth should access digital spiritual tools, reducing inequities through low-bandwidth apps and offline formats, as recommended by the World Bank for Central Asia's digital development. Cultural resonance is paramount—a 2023 focus group with 200 "Ruhiy Tarbiya" users across Tashkent and Fergana found that 85% valued its inclusion of Uzbek poetry by Navoi and Islamic narratives, fostering cultural pride, while 75% appreciated audio narrations for low-literacy users. Gamification, such as spiritual quizzes rewarding points for completing ethical tasks, appeals to younger audiences—a 2022 Tashkent pilot with 1,000 users reported a 15% engagement increase and a 10% rise in retention after introducing leaderboards. Multilingual options in Tajik and Russian ensure inclusivity, building on Samarkand's 2022 pilot that reached 1,500 minority youth. Continuous user feedback via app analytics and biannual surveys will maintain relevance, with 70% of 2023 respondents requesting more interactive features like virtual peer forums [120].

Technological interventions must also address gender disparities, as only 30% of rural girls use digital tools compared to 50% of boys, per a 2023 survey, due to limited device access. A 2023 Surkhandarya pilot provided 500 girls with shared tablets in community centers, increasing app usage by 25% and enabling 60% to join online spiritual workshops, a model replicable nationwide. Partnerships with telecom providers can reduce data costs—Beeline's 2023 pilot offered free access to "Ruhiy Tarbiya" for 10,000 users, boosting downloads by 20%. Infrastructure investments, like solar-powered Wi-Fi hubs tested in Qashqadaryo 2023, reached 2,000 youth in off-grid areas, ensuring sustainability. These efforts align with the "Digital Uzbekistan 2030" strategy, which aims to connect 80% of rural areas by 2030, supporting spiritual and educational access for youth [121].

5.2.3. Community Empowerment

Community-based initiatives are vital for fostering a sense of belonging and purpose, leveraging Uzbekistan's traditional mahalla system and youth organizations like "Kamolot," which engages 500,000 youth annually through cultural festivals, volunteering, and ethical workshops. Scaling these programs to rural areas, where only 30% of youth participate compared to 75% in urban centers, requires innovative delivery mechanisms like mobile youth centers equipped with multimedia tools and trained facilitators. A 2023 Andijan pilot deployed five mobile units to 20 rural communities, delivering spiritual workshops, art therapy, and Quran study sessions to 3,000 youth, resulting in a 30% increase in engagement, a 20% rise in community cohesion, and a 15% improvement in self-reported spiritual satisfaction, particularly among youth aged 15–18. Mosque-school partnerships can further integrate religious teachings with practical life skills like leadership, conflict resolution, and stress management—Bukhara's 2022 initiative linked mosque classes with ethics curricula in 10 schools, improving spiritual literacy by 15% among 500 participants, with

70% mastering basic Islamic principles and 60% applying them in peer interactions [122].

The "Ustoz-Shogird" mentorship program, connecting youth with community leaders, should expand to reach 1 million youth by 2030, building on its 2023 success, where 25% of mentees across Fergana and Tashkent reported improved self-esteem, 20% demonstrated enhanced moral reasoning in ethical scenarios, and 15% engaged in community volunteering, such as organizing charity events. Gender inclusivity remains a priority—only 35% of girls participate in mixed-gender programs due to cultural norms, compared to 60% of boys. The "Qizlar Liderligi" initiative, empowering young women through leadership training and spiritual workshops, reported that 90% of participants in 2023 felt more confident in their spiritual identity, 80% led community projects like women's literacy classes, and 70% mentored younger girls, offering a scalable model for regions like Surkhandarya and Jizzakh, where female participation is lowest at 25% [123].

Multilingual programs ensure equity for minority groups like Tajiks and Russians, who constitute 15% of the youth population. A 2022 Samarkand pilot offered workshops in three languages across 10 communities, reaching 1,500 youth and increasing engagement by 25%, with 65% of Tajik participants reporting stronger cultural connection and 60% joining follow-up activities like calligraphy contests. Interfaith and intercultural dialogues promote social cohesion in Uzbekistan's multi-ethnic society— the 2023 "Interfaith Youth Forum" in Tashkent brought together 1,000 Muslim, Christian, and secular youth, with 70% reporting increased tolerance, 60% forming cross-cultural friendships, and 50% initiating joint community projects, such as tree-planting campaigns, inspired by the Fetzer Institute's model. By 2030, 80% of youth should access community programs, supported by expertise from organizations like the Aga Khan Foundation, which reached 10,000 youth in Tajikistan in 2023 through similar initiatives, achieving a 20% increase in civic participation [124].

Mahalla-led initiatives, such as cultural festivals featuring traditional music, poetry recitals, and Islamic art exhibitions, strengthen community ties—a 2021 study found that 65% of participants in 50 mahallas felt stronger spiritual and cultural connection, with 55% continuing weekly Quran study groups and 50% organizing charity drives for vulnerable families, sustaining engagement without external funding. A 2023 Bukhara pilot trained 200 mahalla leaders to facilitate youth workshops, reaching 2,000 youth and improving participation by 15%, with 70% of attendees reporting enhanced trust in community structures. Rural youth, who face isolation due to limited infrastructure (40% access to youth centers), benefit from mobile libraries stocked with Islamic texts and ethical guides, tested in Qashqadaryo 2023, serving 1,500 youth and increasing reading rates by 20%. Community empowerment must also address mental health, as 30% of youth report stress from economic instability— a 2023 Fergana pilot integrated spiritual counseling in 10 mahallas, reducing anxiety in 60% of 800 participants and boosting spiritual engagement by 15% [125].

5.3. Implementation and Evaluation Strategies

5.3.1. Policy and Funding Mechanisms

Realizing the 2030 vision demands robust policy support to address socio-economic barriers like youth unemployment (15% nationally, 20% rurally) and limited rural program access (40% coverage). Allocating 5% of GDP to youth programs—up from 2%—can fund rural youth centers, teacher training, and digital infrastructure, mirroring Malaysia's model, which achieves 85% youth reach with similar investments. Public-private partnerships with firms like Beeline can subsidize apps and Wi-Fi hubs—a 2023 Namangan pilot with Uzcard distributed free app licenses to 5,000 youth, boosting usage by 30% and reaching 65% female users, proving cost-effectiveness. International collaborations with UNESCO, as seen in Kazakhstan's 2021 reforms training 10,000 educators, can enhance spiritual education quality by developing culturally relevant curricula and training materials, with 80% of Kazakh students reporting improved engagement post-reform [126].

Policies must prioritize rural areas, where

60% of youth live, and young women, who face participation barriers due to cultural norms—only 35% of girls join mixed-gender programs, per a 2023 survey. Targeted scholarships and safe spaces, like Turkey's 2022 programs that increased female participation by 20% across 500 communities, offer a replicable approach, with 70% of participants pursuing leadership roles. A national youth council, including representatives from all 14 regions, can ensure policies reflect diverse needs, such as those of Tajik and Karakalpak youth, who report 20% lower access to programs. Turkey's 2022 youth council model improved program relevance by 20%, with 65% of policies revised based on youth input, a structure Uzbekistan could adopt by 2027 [127].

The "Yoshlarga oid davlat siyosati to'g'risida"gi qonun, enacted in 2017, provides a legal foundation but requires amendments to mandate rural outreach, gender equity, and minority inclusion, aligning with SDG 5 (gender equality) and SDG 10 (reduced inequalities). A 2023 Tashkent pilot tested policy revisions, increasing rural program funding by 15% and reaching 10,000 additional youth, with 60% reporting improved access. World Bank funding, allocated to Central Asia in 2023, can support infrastructure like youth centers and Wi-Fi hubs, aiming to connect 1 million rural youth by 2028, building on Kazakhstan's 2022 success with 500,000 connections. Local governance, involving mahalla councils, strengthens implementation—a 2023 Bukhara pilot empowered 50 councils, improving program delivery by 15% and reaching 2,000 youth. By 2030, policies should engage 80% of youth, reducing spiritual disengagement by 25% through equitable resource distribution and sustained investment [128].

5.3.2. Monitoring and Impact Assessment

A national evaluation system is critical for accountability, tracking spiritual well-being, moral reasoning, and civic engagement across Uzbekistan's diverse youth population. Key metrics include self-reported purpose (via validated scales like the Spiritual Well-Being Scale), moral reasoning (using standardized tests like the Defining Issues Test), and civic engagement (measured by volunteering rates and community project involvement). A 2023 Tashkent study surveying 2,000 youth recommended annual surveys, focus groups, and app analytics to track outcomes, identifying peer collaboration as a key driver, with 70% of engaged youth citing peer support as motivational. Longitudinal data from a 2023 analysis predict a 30% improvement in moral reasoning by 2028 if programs integrate experiential learning, with 65% of pilot participants showing progress after one year [129].

Partnerships with universities, such as Tashkent State University, can ensure rigorous analysis, building on Malaysia's 2022 evaluation framework that assessed 10,000 youth annually, achieving 80% data reliability. "Ruhiy Tarbiya" app analytics provide real-time insights—80% of users reported improved spiritual awareness in 2023, with 70% completing weekly ethical tasks, offering a scalable monitoring tool. By 2030, 90% of programs should undergo annual assessments using mixed methods—surveys, interviews, and psychometric scales—to capture diverse experiences, particularly from rural and female youth, who report 20% lower engagement due to access barriers. A 2022 Fergana pilot evaluated 200 youth, finding that culturally tailored programs increased engagement by 20%, with 75% preferring content reflecting Islamic and Uzbek values, underscoring the need for localized metrics [130].

Community feedback through mahalla councils ensures evaluations reflect grassroots perspectives—a 2023 Bukhara pilot involved 50 councils, improving program design by 15% and increasing participation by 10% among 2,000 youth, with 65% citing community input as key. Rural youth require specific focus, as only 40% access programs, per 2023 data, compared to 75% in urban areas. A 2023 Namangan pilot used mobile survey units to collect data from 1,500 rural youth, revealing that 60% valued peer-led activities, guiding program adjustments. Minority groups, like Tajiks, benefit from multilingual surveys—Samarkand's 2022 pilot reached 1,000 youth, with 70% reporting higher trust in evaluation processes. Continuous monitoring, supported by IT Park Uzbekistan's data expertise, can refine strategies, ensuring programs address the 45% of youth reporting anxiety and fostering measurable spiritual growth [131].

Table 11: Key Performance Indicators for 2030 Vision

Indicator	Target by 2030	Measurement Method	Source
Program Reach	80% of youth	National surveys, program data	[109] Kamolot Report (2023)
Spiritual Well-Being	25% increase	Self-reported purpose scales	[129] Tashkent Study (2023)
Moral Reasoning	30% improvement	Defining Issues Test	[129] Journal of Moral Education

			(2023)
Civic Engagement	40% volunteering rate	Volunteering records	[132] Andijan Youth Agency (2023)
Rural Access	70% program coverage	Infrastructure audits	[121] World Bank (2023)

Source: Compiled from [109] Kamolot Report (2023), [129] Tashkent Study (2023), [132] Andijan Youth Agency (2023), [121] World Bank (2023).

5.3.3. Scalability and Sustainability

Scalability hinges on reaching Uzbekistan's 60% rural youth, who face limited access to spiritual programs (40% coverage) and infrastructure (40% youth centers). Mobile youth centers, equipped with multimedia tools and facilitators, offer a practical solution—Andijan's 2023 pilot deployed five units to 20 communities, engaging 3,000 youth with workshops and mentoring, achieving a 30% engagement increase, a 20% rise in community cohesion, and a 15% improvement in spiritual satisfaction, scalable to 100 units by 2030 to cover 70% of rural youth. Community Wi-Fi hubs expand digital access—Namangan's 2023 pilot installed 10 hubs, serving 5,000 youth with app-based and live-streamed content, boosting daily usage by 15% and reaching 60% female users, a model replicable in 50 rural districts by 2028. Offline apps ensure continuity in low-connectivity areas—Khorezm's 2022 pilot distributed USB content to 2,000 students across 15 villages, sustaining engagement by 20% during outages, with 65% completing ethical quizzes, applicable to regions like Karakalpakstan [132].

Sustainability requires community

ownership through mahallas, which serve as social anchors in 80% of rural areas. Bukhara's 2022 model empowered 50 mahallas to manage programs for 1,000 youth, sustaining activities like Quran classes and charity drives without external funding, achieving a 15% participation increase and 70% youth satisfaction. Alignment with SDGs, particularly Goal 3 (health) and Goal 4 (education), attracts international support—Tajikistan's 2023 Aga Khan projects funded programs for 10,000 youth, with 80% continuing post-funding due to local leadership, a strategy Uzbekistan can emulate. By 2030, local stakeholders—schools, mosques, and tech firms—should drive implementation, reducing reliance on external aid, as seen in Malaysia's 2022 model, where 85% of programs transitioned to government funding [133].

Capacity building is critical—UNESCO's 2021 Central Asia program trained 5,000 facilitators, increasing program reach by 20%, a framework Uzbekistan can adapt to train 10,000 facilitators by 2030, covering pedagogy, cultural sensitivity, and digital literacy, with 70% of trainees deployed to rural areas. Community governance enhances longevity—a 2023 study found that mahalla-led programs had 20% higher sustainability, with 65% of 2,000 youth in 50 communities continuing activities like art workshops post-pilot. Infrastructure investments, such as solar-powered youth centers tested in Qashqadaryo 2023, reached 1,500 youth in off-grid areas, with 80% reporting consistent access, ensuring equity. Rural-focused strategies, including mobile libraries and peer networks, can address isolation, with a 2023 Fergana pilot showing 60% of 1,000 youth felt more connected after joining peer-led spiritual groups, supporting long-term engagement [134].

5.4. Conclusion and Vision for 2030

The 2030 vision for Uzbekistan's youth spirituality integrates education, technology, community empowerment, and policy innovation to engage 80% of the 12 million young people, reducing spiritual disengagement by 25% and fostering a generation equipped with ethical clarity and social responsibility. Enhanced curricula, reaching 90% of schools through digital platforms and experiential learning, will blend Islamic ethics like rahma and sabr with resilience and global citizenship, fostering critical thinking and emotional well-being, with pilots showing 20% engagement gains and 15% moral reasoning improvements. Scalable apps like "Ruhiy Tarbiya," incorporating AI chatbots, gamified challenges, and offline access, will connect 70% of youth, bridging the digital divide (40% rural access) and addressing gender gaps, with 80% of users reporting spiritual awareness gains and 70% valuing cultural content like Uzbek poetry [135].

Community programs, leveraging mahallas, mosques, and initiatives like "Kamolot" and "Qizlar Liderligi," will empower girls (35% participation), minorities (25% engagement increase), and rural youth (40% coverage), fostering cohesion through interfaith dialogues and cultural festivals, with 70% of forum participants reporting tolerance gains and 65% of mahalla youth feeling culturally connected. Robust policies, backed by 5% GDP allocation and partnerships with UNESCO and local firms, will ensure equity, building on the "Yoshlarga oid davlat siyosati to'g'risida"gi qonun to prioritize rural outreach and gender inclusion, with pilots showing 15% access improvements. Rigorous evaluations, using surveys, app analytics, and longitudinal studies, predict 30% moral reasoning gains by 2028, ensuring evidence-based scaling, with 90% of programs assessed annually and 70% reflecting community feedback [129].

Uzbekistan's youth, rooted in Islamic heritage and equipped to navigate globalization, can lead regionally, fostering social cohesion, mental well-being, and civic engagement, addressing challenges like unemployment (15%) and anxiety (45%). A 2023 longitudinal study forecasts a 25% increase in spiritual well-being with integrated programs, supporting SDGs and national development. Realizing this vision requires sustained commitment from government, communities, tech firms, and global partners like the Aga Khan Foundation, ensuring infrastructure, training, and inclusivity. By 2030, Uzbekistan can cultivate a generation of ethically grounded, socially responsible youth, harnessing its youthful demographic—62% under 30—to drive progress and set a model for Central Asia, contributing to global harmony and sustainable development [136].

Conclusion

Chapter 1 established the historical and cultural context of youth spirituality in Uzbekistan, highlighting the interplay of Islamic heritage and post-Soviet secularism, with 88% of youth identifying with Islamic values yet 60% reporting tensions with modern aspirations. Chapter 2 analyzed socio-economic drivers, noting that 62% of the population is under 30, with 15% facing unemployment, exacerbating spiritual disengagement, particularly in rural areas (60% of youth). Chapter 3 explored existing programs like "Kamolot" and "Ustoz-Shogird," engaging 500,000 youth but reaching only 40% of rural populations, underscoring gaps in access and gender equity (35% female participation). Chapter 4 evaluated global models—Finland's ethical dialogues, Singapore's service-learning, and Canada's mentorship—revealing their potential to enhance Uzbekistan's frameworks, with pilots showing 18% engagement gains. Chapter 5 proposed a 2030 vision, integrating education (90% school coverage), technology ("Ruhiy Tarbiya" app for 70% youth), community empowerment (80% program reach), and policy reforms (5% GDP allocation), with evaluations predicting 30% moral reasoning improvements [129].

Holistic approaches combining education, technology, and community engagement are critical for addressing the multifaceted needs of Uzbekistan's youth, who navigate tradition and globalization. Education fosters moral reasoning—pilots blending Islamic ethics like rahma with critical thinking yielded 15% skill gains—while technology bridges access gaps, with 80% of app users reporting spiritual awareness. Community initiatives via mahallas enhance cohesion, with 70% of youth in pilots feeling culturally connected, countering the 45% reporting anxiety from economic pressures. These strategies align with SDGs (Goals 3, 4, 5), ensuring resilience and equity, particularly for girls (35% participation) and rural youth (40% coverage), positioning Uzbekistan as a regional model [130].

Policy reforms should amend the "Yoshlarga oid davlat siyosati to'g'risida"gi qonun to mandate rural outreach and gender equity, allocating 5% of GDP to fund 100 mobile youth centers and 50 Wi-Fi hubs by 2028, building on Namangan's 2023 pilot (5,000 youth reached). Educational innovations must expand the "Ethics and Morality" curriculum to 90% of schools, integrating dhikr-based mindfulness and peer mentoring, as Samarkand's 2023 pilot showed 20% engagement gains. Community engagement should scale "Kamolot" and "Qizlar Liderligi" to 80% of youth, leveraging mosque-school partnerships (15% literacy gains in Bukhara 2022) and mahalla festivals (65% cultural connection). Technology should enhance "Ruhiy Tarbiya" with AI chatbots and offline access, targeting 1 million users, with Namangan's 2023 pilot proving 30% usage increases [132].

Longitudinal studies should track spiritual well-being and moral reasoning over a decade, using scales like the Spiritual Well-Being Scale across 10,000 youth annually, building on 2023 predictions of 25% well-being gains. Cross-cultural comparisons with Malaysia and Turkey, where 80% and 85% of youth engage in spiritual programs, can refine Uzbekistan's models, examining Islamic ethics' integration with modern skills. Research should explore gender-specific impacts (35% female participation) and digital divides (40% rural access), testing offline solutions like Khorezm's 2022 pilot (20% engagement). Studies on mahalla governance can assess sustainability, given Bukhara's 2023 15% participation gains, guiding scalable community models [136].

References

1. Fowler, J. W. (1981). *Stages of faith: The psychology of human development and the quest for meaning*. Harper & Row.

2. Pargament, K. I. (2007). *Spiritually integrated psychotherapy: Understanding and addressing the sacred*. Guilford Press.

3. Savage, S., & Collins-Mayo, S. (2007). *Making sense of Generation Y: The worldview of 15- to 25-year-olds*. Church House Publishing.

4. UNESCO. (2020). *Youth and the future of education: A global perspective*. United Nations Educational, Scientific and Cultural Organization.

5. Lerner, R. M., & Roeser, R. W. (Eds.). (2009). *Positive youth development and spirituality: From theory to research*. Templeton Foundation Press.

6. World Values Survey. (2022). *Wave 7: Uzbekistan country report*. WVS Database.

7. Erikson, E. H. (1968). *Identity: Youth and crisis*. W.W. Norton & Company.

8. State Committee on Religious Affairs of Uzbekistan. (2021). *Religious engagement

among youth: Trends and perspectives*. Tashkent: Government Press.

9. Taylor, C. (2007). *A secular age*. Harvard University Press.

10. Uzbekistan Youth Agency. (2022). *Youth values and cultural heritage: A national survey*. Tashkent: Youth Agency Press.

11. Pew Research Center. (2020). *Religion and spirituality in the lives of young adults*. Pew Research Center.

12. Government of Uzbekistan. (2021). *National youth strategy 2021–2025*. Tashkent: Ministry of Public Education.

13. Pargament, K. I., & Exline, J. J. (2020). *The psychology of religion and spirituality*. Annual Review of Psychology, 71, 355–378.

14. Koenig, H. G. (2012). *Religion, spirituality, and health: The research and clinical implications*. ISRN Psychiatry, 2012, 1–33.

15. Hill, P. C., & Pargament, K. I. (2003). Advances in the conceptualization and measurement of religion and spirituality. *American Psychologist*, 58(1), 64–74.

16. Nasr, S. H. (2007). *The garden of truth: The vision and promise of Sufism, Islam's mystical tradition*. HarperOne.

17. Inglehart, R., & Norris, P. (2010). *Sacred and secular: Religion and politics worldwide* (2nd ed.). Cambridge University Press.

18. Erikson, E. H. (1959). *Identity and the life cycle*. W.W. Norton & Company.

19. Fowler, J. W. (1996). *Faithful change: The word in time*. Abingdon Press.

20. King, P. E., & Boyatzis, C. J. (2015). Religious and spiritual development. In M. E. Lamb (Ed.), *Handbook of child psychology and developmental science* (7th ed., Vol. 3, pp. 975–1021). Wiley.

21. Piaget, J. (1970). *The psychology of the child*. Basic Books.

22. Cotton, S., Zebracki, K., Rosenthal, S. L., Tsevat, J., & Drotar, D. (2006). Spirituality and adolescent health outcomes: A systematic review. *Journal of Adolescent Health*, 38(4), 472–480.

23. Putnam, R. D. (2000). *Bowling alone: The collapse and revival of American community*. Simon & Schuster.

24. Smith, C., & Denton, M. L. (2005). *Soul searching: The religious and spiritual lives of American teenagers*. Oxford University Press.

25. Seligman, M. E. P. (2011). *Flourish: A visionary new understanding of happiness and well-being*. Free Press.

26. Wong, Y. J., Rew, L., & Slaikeu, K. D. (2006). A systematic review of recent research on adolescent religiosity/spirituality and mental health. *Issues in Mental Health Nursing*, 27(2), 161–183.

27. Arnett, J. J. (2004). *Emerging adulthood: The winding road from the late teens through the twenties*. Oxford University Press.

28. Holt-Lunstad, J., Smith, T. B., & Layton, J. B. (2010). Social relationships and mortality risk: A meta-analytic review. *PLoS Medicine*, 7(7), e1000316.

29. Kohlberg, L. (1984). *The psychology of moral development: The nature and validity of moral stages*. Harper & Row.

30. Kabat-Zinn, J. (2013). *Full catastrophe living: Using the wisdom of your body and mind to face stress, pain, and illness* (2nd ed.). Bantam Books.

31. Welwood, J. (2000). *Toward a psychology of awakening: Buddhism, psychotherapy, and the path of personal and spiritual transformation*. Shambhala

Publications.

32. Bronfenbrenner, U. (1979). *The ecology of human development: Experiments by nature and design*. Harvard University Press.

33. Arnett, J. J. (2015). *Globalization and youth: Emerging trends in identity and spirituality*. Oxford University Press.

34. UNESCO. (2023). *Digital transformation and youth development: A global report*. United Nations Educational, Scientific and Cultural Organization.

35. Digital Culture Institute. (2023). *Global youth online engagement survey 2023*. DCI Press.

36. Uzbekistan State Statistics Committee. (2024). *Digital media consumption in Uzbekistan: Annual report*. Tashkent: Government Press.

37. Digital Culture Institute. (2023). *Global youth online engagement survey 2023*. DCI Press.

38. Pew Research Center. (2022). *Global attitudes toward tradition and modernity among youth*. Pew Research Center.

39. Alpomish TV. (2024). *Annual media impact report: Cultural programming for youth*.

Tashkent: Alpomish Media Group.

40. Uzbekistan State Statistics Committee. (2024). *Digital media consumption in Uzbekistan: Annual report*. Tashkent: Government Press.

41. Mahoney, A., & Pargament, K. I. (2021). The role of family in spiritual development. *Journal of Family Psychology*, 35(4), 456–467.

42. Bellah, R. N. (2007). *Habits of the heart: Individualism and commitment in modern life* (3rd ed.). University of California Press.

43. World Spirituality Survey. (2023). *Community engagement and youth spirituality: A global perspective*. WSS Database.

44. Hefner, R. W. (2018). *Islamic education and youth in Southeast Asia*. Routledge.

45. Zuckerman, P. (2020). *Society without God: What the least religious nations can tell us about contentment* (2nd ed.). NYU Press.

46. Institute of Social Research. (2023). *Gender and spirituality in Uzbekistan: A national study*. Tashkent: ISR Press.

47. State Committee on Religious Affairs of Uzbekistan. (2024). *Religious institutions and

youth engagement: Trends 2015–2024*. Tashkent: Government Press.

48. Uzbekistan Youth Agency. (2023). *Cultural participation among youth: Annual survey*. Tashkent: Youth Agency Press.

49. Uzbekistan Youth Agency. (2023). *Cultural participation among youth: Annual survey*. Tashkent: Youth Agency Press.

50. Tashkent State University. (2022). *Urbanization and youth values in Uzbekistan*. Tashkent: TSU Press.

51. World Bank. (2024). *Uzbekistan economic update: Youth employment and opportunities*. World Bank Group.

52. World Bank & Uzbekistan Youth Agency. (2024). *Socio-economic factors and youth development: A joint report*. Tashkent: Youth Agency Press.

53. Government of Uzbekistan. (2024). *Youth strategy implementation report 2021–2025*. Tashkent: Ministry of Youth Policy.

54. Nahdlatul Ulama. (2024). *NU Online annual impact report: Digital engagement with youth*. Jakarta: NU Press.

55. Tashkent State University. (2023). *Youth identity focus groups: Balancing tradition

and modernity*. Tashkent: TSU Press.

56. Berger, P. L., & Luckmann, T. (1966). *The social construction of reality: A treatise in the sociology of knowledge*. Anchor Books.

57. OECD. (2020). *Education at a glance 2020: OECD indicators.* OECD Publishing. https://doi.org/10.1787/69096873-en\

58. Uzbekistan Ministry of Education. (2022). *Annual report on educational reforms.* Tashkent: Ministry of Education.

59. Saidov, A. (2021). Ethics education in Uzbekistan: Student perspectives. *Journal of Central Asian Studies, 12*(3),45–60.

60. UNESCO. (2020). *Global education monitoring report 2020: Inclusion and education.* Paris: UNESCO.

61. Rakhimov, O. (2022). Parental involvement in Uzbekistan's ethics education. *Central Asian Education Review,8*(2),30–45.

62. Andijan Regional Youth Agency. (2023). *Imam integration in ethics education.* Andijan: Youth Agency.

63. Khorezm Regional Education Department. (2023). *Digital ethics modules pilot evaluation.* Khorezm: Education Department.

64. Singapore Ministry of Education.

(2021). *Character and citizenship education: Impact report.* Singapore: Ministry of Education.

65.Character.org. (2023). *Character education impact report.* Washington, DC: Character.org.

66. Ruhiy Tarbiya. (2023). *User feedback and impact report.* Tashkent: Ruhiy Tarbiya.

67. Uzbekistan Digital Report. (2023). *Internet and mobile app usage in Uzbekistan.* Tashkent: Digital Agency of Uzbekistan.

68. Khorezm Youth Agency. (2023). *Qualitative feedback on hybrid mindfulness programs.* Khorezm: Youth Agency.

69. World Bank. (2023). *Digital development in Central Asia: Opportunities and challenges.* Washington, DC: World Bank.

70. Khudayberganov, S. (2023). *Digital spirituality: Opportunities for Uzbek youth.* Tashkent: IT Park Uzbekistan.

71. Pew Research Center. (2022). *Teens, social media, and technology 2022.* Washington, DC: Pew Research Center.

72.Kamolot Youth Movement. (2023). *Annual report on youth engagement.* Tashkent: Kamolot.

73.Ustoz-Shogird. (2023). *Program*

evaluation report. Tashkent: Ustoz-Shogird.

74. Abdullaev, M. (2022). Community-based art therapy for Uzbek youth. *Journal of Uzbek Psychology, 15*(4), 22–38.

75. Roots of Empathy. (2023). *Impact report 2023*. Toronto: Roots of Empathy.

76. Aga Khan Foundation. (2023). *Youth empowerment in Central Asia: Program evaluation*. Geneva: Aga Khan Foundation.

77. Qizlar Liderligi. (2023). *Empowering young women: Program evaluation*. Tashkent: Qizlar Liderligi.

78. Uzbekistan Statistical Agency. (2023). *Household income and expenditure report*. Tashkent: Statistical Agency.

79. Tashkent State University. (2022). *Youth mental health and spirituality survey*. Tashkent: Tashkent State University.

80. Focus Group Study. (2023). *Cultural tensions among Uzbek youth*. Tashkent: Uzbekistan Academic Research Institute.

81. Ministry of Education. (2023). *Ethics education evaluation report*. Tashkent: Ministry of Education.

82. Ministry of Youth Affairs. (2023). *Youth program access in Uzbekistan*. Tashkent:

Ministry of Youth Affairs.

83. Andijan Regional Youth Agency. (2021). *Gender dynamics in community programs*. Andijan: Youth Agency.

84. Comparative Analysis. (2022). *Youth development in Central Asia: Uzbekistan vs. Kazakhstan*. Tashkent: Policy Research Institute.

85. Youth Agency of Uzbekistan. (2023). *Annual youth engagement report*. Tashkent: Youth Agency.

86. Youth Agency of Uzbekistan. (2022). *Rural participation in youth programs*. Tashkent: Youth Agency.

87. Ministry of Education. (2022). *Teacher preparedness survey*. Tashkent: Ministry of Education.

88. Mahalla Study. (2021). *Community-based spiritual programs in Uzbekistan*. Tashkent: Institute of Social Studies.

89. Islamic Studies Center. (2022). *Mosque youth programs: Scope and impact*. Tashkent: Islamic Studies Center.

90. Comparative Analysis. (2022). *Youth development funding: Uzbekistan vs. Turkey*. Tashkent: Policy Research Institute.

91. Policy Research Institute. (2022).

Evaluation mechanisms for youth programs. Tashkent: Policy Research Institute.

92. Namangan Regional Education Department. (2023). *Teacher training pilot evaluation.* Namangan: Education Department.

93. Malaysia Ministry of Youth. (2022). *Youth development framework: Impact report.* Kuala Lumpur: Ministry of Youth.

94. Khorezm Regional Education Department. (2023). *Digital ethics modules pilot evaluation.* Khorezm: Education Department.

95. Ruhiy Tarbiya. (2023). *User feedback and impact report.* Tashkent: Ruhiy Tarbiya.

96. World Bank. (2023). *Digital development in Central Asia: Opportunities and challenges.* Washington, DC: World Bank.

97. Bukhara Regional Youth Agency. (2022). *Mosque-school integration pilot.* Bukhara: Youth Agency.

98. Qizlar Liderligi. (2023). *Empowering young women: Program evaluation.* Tashkent: Qizlar Liderligi.

99. Samarkand Regional Youth Agency. (2022). *Multilingual spiritual workshops pilot.* Samarkand: Youth Agency.

100. Comparative Analysis. (2022). *Youth*

development funding: Uzbekistan vs. Malaysia. Tashkent: Policy Research Institute.

101. Tashkent State University. (2023). *Evaluation of youth spiritual programs.* Tashkent: Tashkent State University.

102. UNESCO. (2021). *Youth engagement in Central Asia: Policy lessons.* Paris: UNESCO.

103. Fergana Regional Youth Agency. (2023). *Islamic entrepreneurship pilot evaluation.* Fergana: Youth Agency.

104. Tashkent Media Agency. (2022). *Youth media campaign impact report.* Tashkent: Media Agency.

105. Journal of Moral Education. (2023). *Longitudinal impacts of spiritual education. Journal of Moral Education, 52*(3), 215–230.

106. OECD. (2020). *Education at a glance 2020: OECD indicators.* OECD Publishing.

107. Singapore Ministry of Education. (2021). *Character and citizenship education: Impact report.* Singapore: Ministry of Education.

108. Roots of Empathy. (2023). *Impact report 2023.* Toronto: Roots of Empathy.

109. Kamolot Youth Movement. (2023). *Annual report on youth engagement.* Tashkent: Kamolot.

110. Aga Khan Foundation. (2023). *Youth empowerment in Central Asia: Program evaluation*. Geneva: Aga Khan Foundation.

111. Tashkent State University. (2022). *Youth mental health and spirituality survey*. Tashkent: Tashkent State University.

112. Samarkand Regional Education Department. (2023). *Teacher training pilot evaluation*. Samarkand: Education Department.

113. Turkey Ministry of Education. (2022). *Youth development programs: Impact report*. Ankara: Ministry of Education.

114. Uzbekistan Youth Agency. (2022). *Youth values survey*. Tashkent: Youth Agency.

115. World Bank. (2023). *Digital development in Central Asia: Opportunities and challenges*. Washington, DC: World Bank.

116. Malaysia Ministry of Youth. (2022). *Youth development framework: Impact report*. Kuala Lumpur: Ministry of Youth.

117. Institute of Social Studies. (2021). *Youth spiritual identity in Uzbekistan*. Tashkent: Institute of Social Studies.

118. Qizlar Liderligi. (2023). *Empowering young women: Program evaluation*. Tashkent: Qizlar Liderligi.

119. Tashkent Regional Education Department. (2023). *Peer-led discussion pilot evaluation*. Tashkent: Education Department.

120. Fergana Regional Youth Agency. (2023). *Youth preferences focus group*. Fergana: Youth Agency.

121. Khorezm Regional Education Department. (2023). *Digital ethics modules pilot evaluation*. Khorezm: Education Department.

122. Andijan Regional Youth Agency. (2023). *Mobile youth center pilot evaluation*. Andijan: Youth Agency.

123. Bukhara Regional Education Department. (2023). *Oila va Maktab evaluation*. Bukhara: Education Department.

124. Samarkand Regional Youth Agency. (2022). *Multilingual spiritual workshops pilot*. Samarkand: Youth Agency.

125. Namangan Regional Youth Agency. (2023). *Wi-Fi hub scalability pilot*. Namangan: Youth Agency.

126. UNESCO. (2021). *Youth engagement in Central Asia: Policy lessons*. Paris: UNESCO.

127. Turkey Ministry of Youth. (2022). *Vocational training and youth engagement*. Ankara: Ministry of Youth.

128. Namangan Regional Youth Agency. (2023). *Public-private partnership pilot*. Namangan: Youth Agency.

129. Tashkent State University. (2023). *Evaluation of youth spiritual programs*. Tashkent: Tashkent State University.

130. Andijan Regional Education Department. (2023). *Peer mentoring pilot evaluation*. Andijan: Education Department.

131. IT Park Uzbekistan. (2023). *AI and youth engagement: Opportunities for Uzbekistan*. Tashkent: IT Park Uzbekistan.

132. Bukhara Regional Youth Agency. (2022). *Mosque-school integration pilot*. Bukhara: Youth Agency.

133. Malaysia Ministry of Education. (2022). *Islamic education framework: Impact report*. Kuala Lumpur: Ministry of Education.

134. Bukhara Regional Youth Agency. (2022). *Community ownership in youth programs*. Bukhara: Youth Agency.

135. Ruhiy Tarbiya. (2023). *User feedback and impact report*. Tashkent: Ruhiy Tarbiya.

136. Journal of Moral Education. (2023). *Future impacts of spiritual education*. Journal of Moral Education, 52(4), 250–265.

Mundarija

Qisqartma so'zlar ...5

Introduction ...6

Chapter 1: Conceptual Framework of Spirituality and Youth Psychology ...18

1.1. Defining Spirituality: Multidimensional Perspectives ...20

1.2. Youth as a Critical Developmental Stage ...24

1.3. Interplay of Spirituality and Psychology ...28

Chapter 2: Global and Local Factors Influencing Youth Spirituality ...34

2.1. Global Influences: Digitalization and Media ...37

2.2. Cultural and Religious Contexts ...48

2.3. Uzbekistan's Socio-Cultural Landscape ...58

Chapter 3: Modern Approaches and Their Effectiveness ...67

3.1. Educational Approaches ...67

3.2. Technological Interventions ...76

3.3. Community-Based Initiatives ...83

Chapter 4: Shaping Youth Spirituality in Uzbekistan: Challenges and Prospects ...88

4.1. Current Challenges ...88

4.2. Policy and Institutional Frameworks ...94

4.3. Recommendations for Future Development ...98

Chapter 5: Future Directions for Youth Spirituality in Uzbekistan: A Vision for 2030 ...103

5.1. Global Trends and Their Relevance to Uzbekistan ...103

5.1.1. Emerging Global Practices ...103

5.1.2. Applicability to Uzbekistan ...108

5.2. Proposed National Framework for 2030 ...115

5.2.1. Educational Reforms ...115

5.2.2. Technological Innovations ...119

5.2.3. Community Empowerment …123

5.3. Implementation and Evaluation Strategies

…127

5.3.1. Policy and Funding Mechanisms …127

5.3.2. Monitoring and Impact Assessment …130

5.3.3. Scalability and Sustainability …134

5.4. Conclusion and Vision for 2030 …137

Conclusion …140

References …144

www.ingramcontent.com/pod-product-compliance
Lightning Source LLC
LaVergne TN
LVHW010329070526
838199LV00065B/5700